BRAND YOU

QB Darla

AUTHOR • SPEAKER • FRIEND

https://wittypublications.com/

DEDICATION

This book is dedicated to my three sons, Collin, Gavin, and Rian. It is also dedicated to all of the children that I've met on this journey who have passed away or are still battling childhood cancer and other illnesses. It is dedicated to my family, friends, and followers who make this journey possible. Thank you all from the bottom of my heart.

ACKNOWLEDGMENT

Thank you to my mom, dad, sister, niece, nephew, and three sons for their unwavering support throughout the years. Thank you to my teachers, friends, and mentors who have played a part in my life. Thank you to my followers and fans who allow me to inspire them through my words and videos over the years. Thank you to God for allowing me to utilize my gifts for a greater purpose to inspire others.

ABOUT THE AUTHOR

Darla Hall, widely known as "QB Darla," is a dynamic motivational speaker, entrepreneur, and author whose journey from small-town Indiana to national impact is both inspiring and heartwarming.

Hailing from Cloverdale, Indiana, Darla's early life was shaped by strong family values and a deep-rooted sense of community. Her parents instilled in her the importance of resilience and independence, qualities that would later define her professional endeavors. Growing up, she was often reminded that "dynamite comes in small packages," a testament to her vibrant energy and determination. She was given the nickname "Mighty Mo" at an early age as she played sports.

In 2012, a life-changing event propelled Darla into entrepreneurship. After a young boy named Miles was struck by a car, Darla sought the perfect gift to uplift his spirits during recovery. Unable to find a suitable option, she took matters into her own hands, creating the first-ever team-themed activity book. This heartfelt gesture marked the inception of "In the Sports Zone," a company dedicated to producing engaging activity books for children. Over the years, Darla expanded her offerings to include over 200 sports teams and donated over 50,000 books to hospitalized children nationwide.

Beyond her entrepreneurial pursuits, Darla serves as Market Manager at Frontdoor, where she continues to build meaningful relationships and drive positive change.

As a motivational speaker, QB Darla captivates audiences with her authenticity and passion. Her talks emphasize the importance of maintaining a positive mindset, striving for balance, and embracing one's unique journey. Drawing from personal experiences and challenges, she encourages individuals to "throw a touchdown" in their own lives, symbolizing the pursuit of personal and professional goals.

Darla's literary contributions further reflect her commitment to empowerment and education. Her works include a range of Witty & Friends activity books for children and "Matters of a Positive Mindset," a workbook that helps adults with personal development and resilience.

In all her endeavors, QB Darla remains dedicated to making a difference, one interaction at a time. She is a proud mom of three sons, Collin, Gavin, and Rian. Her story serves as a testament to the impact of compassion, creativity, and unwavering determination.

AUTHOR • SPEAKER • FRIEND

https://wittypublications.com/

TABLE OF CONTENTS

PREFACE

Believe in yourself, build your personal brand, spread kindness, take action, and achieve great things!

I've been preparing my mind and my heart for a long time to share how I'm able to reach sheer happiness with a balanced life of love and kindness while building my brand to help as many people believe in themselves as possible. I want to impact the world and shower people with hope and motivation to not only chase after their dreams but also attain them with grit and determination.

Anyone who knows me or who has followed me on Facebook, LinkedIn, Instagram, or TikTok knows that I truly want to see others succeed. The three greatest compliments I could get are "she is a great mom," she works hard," and "she shines when she helps others achieve success in their own unique way."

Whether you are a mom or dad, an entrepreneur, a businessperson, a millionaire, a blue-collar worker, or a young adult trying to find your way in life, this book will give you the mindset and tools necessary to take action. It won't be just a lot of smack talk and big ideas that very few can accomplish. It will be real talk, tangible ideas, action items, inspiration, and great vibes. It's time to level up your attitude, your ambitions, and your impact on the world. Most importantly, you'll learn to do it for the right reasons to make the world a better place for generations to come.

Every single person is their own unique brand. Yes, a stay-at-home mom or dad has a brand. A child has their own brand. A millionaire has his/her brand. A realtor or any entrepreneur has their own brand. An influencer has their own brand. If you are breathing, you have your own brand.

Now, what you do with that, if anything, is up to you. You never know just how many eyes are watching your daily actions or content. Know that people are watching, listening, and learning at all times in this digital age we are in.

Social media has changed the world we live in. Back in the day, we didn't have fancy cell phones, digital books, podcasts, YouTube, Facebook, Instagram, TikTok, Twitter, or LinkedIn. We looked out the windows when we went on road trips and appreciated the scenic route. We didn't have GPS, AI, or the internet. We led more private lives. We had conversations, built relationships, and socialized face to face. We would get lost because we didn't have a GPS to define every turn. Getting lost is not always a bad thing. You can discover new things when you get lost as long as you eventually find your way. Life is the same way. Oftentimes, we take different paths and make mistakes, but eventually get back on the right path.

This book is a powerful one-two punch on how to define BRAND YOU (insert your name here), build your personal brand, and maximize your opportunities. It will help you avoid pitfalls and mistakes as you move through your journey. It will make you laugh, cry, and find a healthy balance.

Building Brand YOU is not being boastful or arrogant in this endeavor. Building your own brand will help you:

-Search for a job

-Inspire others

-Find your passion

-Get a raise

-Make bold business moves

-Sell more

-Make more money

-Find joy

-Believe in yourself

-Reach your goals

-Be a better person

-Impact the world in your own unique way

-Love more

-Explore

I want to thank my three sons, my parents, and anyone who has believed in me along my journey. I want to thank the parents who let me into the lives of their children who were going through cancer and other illnesses. I want to thank those of you who follow me on social media and allow me to sprinkle positivity into your lives. I want to encourage everyone to find someone who needs a helping hand and give them whatever you can. I love you all! I truly want you to use this book to WIN!

ABOUT ME

Darla Hall is a mom, a sister, a daughter, and a believer. A believer in God, a believer in you, a believer in hard work, and a believer in living life to the fullest every single day. I could write books on many different topics, and I chose this one because I believe that everyone can benefit from working on their personal brand.

When I was growing up in Belle Union, Indiana, we didn't have cell phones, GPS, or social media. The only type of role models we knew were our parents, coaches, and teachers at school. Luckily, I had some good coaches like Connie Clearwater and Becky Brothers. Coach Clearwater taught me that even when the girls moved in because they thought I didn't have the power to hit the ball, I could knock it over their heads and gain their respect. She gave me the nickname "Mighty Moe," and I went on to play on many top-tier travel teams around the state. Coach Brothers taught me that even though I was 4'11 and 3/4" tall, I could still start on Varsity and play front row. I just had to jump higher. So my dad put up a piece of tape on the wall, and I jumped, and jumped, and jumped until I did just that! I earned All-County, All-Conference, and our small team from South Putnam High School became a force to be reckoned with. I had always been raised to be respectful of others, to love God, and to treat others the way I wanted to be treated. Homecoming Queen was an honor for me because it was voted on, and that meant that I tried my best to include others. I put in effort to try to stay out of drama and turned my attention to competition and sports instead. I had one crush in high school, and he never paid attention to me. That was a good, hearty serving of humble pie.

My parents worked hard to pay for all of my sports throughout the years. After sports, I was determined to take my creativity and determination to the workforce.

I don't want to bore you, but I think it's important for you to know my heart and my foundation to lay the groundwork for how my personal brand came about. It could help you understand one way a personal brand can just sneak up on you and find you!

Bear with me because the rest of this book is going to be about YOU, how to build your personal brand, how to grow your following, tactics to implement, understanding the power you can have to influence other people's lives, and so much more.

I graduated from Ball State University, where I cheered for four years, joined Alpha Gamma Delta, and earned a Bachelor's Degree in Public Relations with a Marketing minor. I had no idea what I was going to do with my knowledge, but I was determined to make money and provide a good life for my family. At that time, I was not thinking that I would build a platform to help thousands of people. That didn't even cross my mind.

I got pregnant and had my first child at 21 and felt very blessed. I knew I wanted to work hard to provide for my family. I also wanted to set a good example of success for them. I went on to have two more sons and loved being a mom. My relationships were filled with ups and downs because I always had ants in my pants. I was driven and competitive, and had big goals to be successful in my career. I knew that I was built to endure hardships in order to become EXTRAORDINARY. I wouldn't be satisfied with the status quo. I wanted to be a small-town girl who made some kind of impact in the world. I didn't know exactly what that would be...yet!

I was Darla Parker, a young lady finding her way in life... one day, one struggle, one learning experience at a time.

I loved my career path, starting in Ball State Sports Information with my first boss, Joe Hernandez. I applied for my first real job and forgot to put my name on my resume. Luckily, the guy liked my resume enough to call my old boss to track me down. That was my first experience with personal branding, and I didn't even realize it. I started as an intern and was quickly promoted to Assistant Director of PR and Employee of the Year for the Amateur Athletic Union. I showed up early and left late. If I didn't know something, I asked how to do it. I learned as I went.

When they moved to Orlando, I decided to stay in Indiana and look for my next adventure. I applied for a few jobs, and then I saw a posting for a big box retail chain called Incredible Universe, owned by Tandy Corporation. I applied with confidence and had a marketing plan written before I got a call back for the first interview. I went in as if I were already hired with a game plan ready to execute. I knew I had to be different and stand apart from the thousands who were vying for the highly sought-after position. I got the job and was quickly promoted to Eastern Region Marketing Manager. I had a blast until one day, they decided to close down all stores. I didn't waste any time as I accepted a job as Marketing Manager for Adam's Mark Hotels. Five years into that job, I got antsy and applied for a job with MZD Advertising. There, I won Employee of the Year and went from Account Executive to Director of New Business Development. Ten years later, I moved to Alabama and enjoyed being a stay-at-home mom for a couple of years, watching my boys grow up, playing tennis, and being involved in their schools.

Then, I got the itch to go back to work, so I started my own advertising agency called HallMarketing. I created business and marketing strategies for small to mid-sized companies. One day in 2012, I was supposed to have a marketing meeting with Burdette Dental Lab. As I called to confirm, he didn't answer. I spoke to his secretary, who told me that his son had just been struck by a car and he was on his way to the hospital. My heart broke. I went immediately into prayer mode. I remembered that his dad said he loved Alabama football, so I went out searching for a gift for him. I couldn't find what I was looking for, as I wanted something he could do while he was in the hospital recovering from two broken legs. I stayed up that night until 3 a.m. sketching out a Roll Tide Activity Book that would be this 8-year-old boy's gift. I had to get him something else, but little did he know that gift would be a work in progress over the next year, that he would get the very first edition. It was a creative piece that I would go on to touch 50,000 plus kids' lives by donating them to children who had illnesses in hospitals throughout the country. Wow...What a journey that started! My heart would forever be changed. I didn't create this product to make money. I created it to help kids. I would go on to sell $1.4M in activity books for 32 college teams, 30 NFL teams, 30 NBA teams, NASCAR, and 32 MLB teams. These sales helped me grow a business to pay myself a salary and donate more books to put smiles on kids' faces. Then, covid hit, and I had to pivot.

The licensing business was tough, so I decided to create my own brand of activity books called Witty & Friends. I established Witty Publications and still do some activity books for teams to continue donating books. I met many amazing kids over those years who inspired me. I love them all and have so many stories to share about how they were so incredibly brave. I'll share a few in the chapters of this book. The parents of these kids encouraged me to start sharing my stories to inspire others. This is where QB Darla, my personal brand, was born. I was speaking for a group of 200, and one of the audience members said, "You're kinda like a quarterback for people's lives," to which I answered, "Yes, I guess I am. I like to help kids and people throw their own touchdowns!"

So...from that day forward, my brand found me, and it stuck. I knew I had to continue to motivate others because I was their QB, their play caller, their motivator, their hype girl!

I recently secured my real estate broker license and am currently the Market Manager for Frontdoor in Indiana. I also continue to do marketing consulting and writing songs, books, and speaking. I'm a part owner in a medical device company in which I've helped get from a drawing to a patented product ready to go to market. I have incorporated my personal brand into everything that I do. I continue to do motivational speaking and workshops to help others. In this book, I'll show you how you can use your personal brand to help build sales for a larger company. Corporations should welcome individuals who have the desire to impact their communities through their own personal brands.

Down, set, hike! Get ready to throw your own touchdown and build your own personal brand!

Bonus in the back of the book: Motivation from QB Darla is a compilation of motivational writings over the years.

CHAPTER 1

What is a Brand?

I would like to set the stage and talk about the definition of a brand and then offer my own thoughts about personal branding.

According to Wikipedia, a brand is a name, symbol, design, term, or other feature that distinguishes a product or service from others. Brands are used in marketing, advertising, and business to create value and recognition for a brand's customers, owners, and shareholders.

· **Personal branding**: The perception or impression of an individual based on their expertise, experience, actions, achievements, and competencies.

Now, I'm going to give you my opinion of what a personal brand is. A personal brand can encompass many things—some positive, some less so. Every single individual is unique, so every single personal brand will be different. There is a 1 in 64 billion chance that you have the same fingerprint as someone else. That's great news for you. You have the ability to own your unique personality and shine in the way only you can.

You may like some people's personal brand or you may not. The beauty of social media is that you get to choose the content you follow. If you don't like something, the kind thing to do is to set your preferences to see less of it. There is no need to troll or say negative things to people, you never know whose that might impact their well-being. The world is full of negative people, so I'd like to encourage more positivity. Compliments on the content go a long way. Once you say something negative, it's not easy to take it back. Why lose sleep over your satisfaction to dig at someone and make them feel bad? If you don't have anything good to say, don't say it. There are ways you can vent and appease yourself, but sitting behind a screen and trolling people is not brave, and it's not necessary.

Your personal brand needs to be something that you define if you intend to grow a following, generate more sales, land a job, influence others, or strive to build a community of supporters.

Here are a few types of content creators:

1-Fake it till you make it

I'm not a fan of this philosophy when it comes to building your personal brand. People want to get to know the real you.

It's important to be authentic. Show your true colors. Show your mistakes. People relate to someone who is real. If you're fake, typically, people see right through it, or it's revealed at some point. Don't be afraid to make fun of yourself, and allow the audience to connect with you and your flaws. Success is many times in the eye of the beholder, so don't try to be someone you're not to fool the viewers. They will learn more if they see a rags-to-riches story unfold.

Some people hire outside sources to build their brands. Oftentimes, these people build it with algorithms that push posts out. This can be good or bad. These companies should be researched carefully because you don't want a bunch of strangers who aren't targeted to your goals. Having fewer followers who are real and engaged is better than having a ton of fake accounts that don't engage and benefit from your content.

Your personality, your upbringing, your faith, your friends, your life choices, your education, your intelligence, your job, your talents, and many other factors play into what your personal brand becomes to the outside world.

2- Born to be Wild

Some are born into celebrity status, or work hard to gain it through movie deals, getting signed by a music label, or getting published if you're an author or speaker. It does speed up the exposure and makes marketing much easier this way. If you weren't born into wealth, don't worry. Happiness is not determined by money or wealth.

3- Grit & Talent

Everyone has gifts to share with the world. Some find them and share them publicly, and some don't. It's a choice you have now with the power of social media. This is how the ones who have talents can make it even if a big company turns them down. The music industry is a great example of this. Kane Brown, Walker Hayes, and many musicians have been turned down by the music industry and found fans through social channels. There are thousands of talented individuals who are more talented than the stars performing on social platforms for the world to enjoy. They may be struggling to make money, but they are trying, so we should support them.

4- Show me the Money

Some people who push their brand are in it for the money. They have chosen to make a career out of trying to build their followers, creating content to get paid, or getting brand or advertising deals. Their content is heavily about showcasing products and getting paid as others shop in their stores or use their discount codes.

5-In It to Win It

Some people are in it for the sheer satisfaction of competing against other influencers, selling more than others, and building a bigger empire than others. Competition is healthy, and sometimes, that is what drives success. Keep it healthy, so your actions don't hurt others.

6- Look, ma, I'm famous!

Some have the desire to be famous, so they go to great lengths to go viral. They want as many followers and likes as they can get. They want to see their name on billboards and shining in the bright lights.

7- AH-HA!

Some will follow a path in life where their personal brand finds them. They may not want to make millions from it. They may just want to help others through positive messaging or inspiration. They just want to make the world a better place.

8- Nope, not I!

Some do not care at all about their personal brand. They don't think it's important, and they don't need it. They like to keep their lives private and not share anything publicly. And... that's OK.

9- *Unknowns*

Some have a personal brand and don't even realize it. When you are going to a job interview, you prepare a resume that showcases your skills and abilities. You are, in a sense, starting to build your personal brand when you do that. You're trying to sell yourself to a company to hire you. Leaders have a personal brand even if they don't use social media. They are admired and looked up to by their employees. Business owners have a personal brand and a corporate brand. People aspire to be in their position, and they are watched.

10- *Dual Brands*

Some people are bound to the rules and regulations of their corporate brand that take precedence over their own personal brand. If your personal brand will help your corporate brand, you may need to talk to your superiors to get permission to utilize your strengths. Many people are working full-time jobs, along with a weekend side hustle, these days to make ends meet. Corporations should realize the power of positive personal brands in helping with productivity and sales.

And...sometimes there is a combination of any of the above.

It's not easy to create consistent content, so I applaud you if you are a content creator.

You don't have to put an identity to your brand like "QB Darla." It helps with consistency in your communications, but it can be a graphic look and feel, a way you communicate and present yourself, or just simply something that you strive to be and no one else can tell.

As long as your intention is to help others and not build it to hurt others, a personal brand can be good. If used to make the world a better place, it can be GREAT! It's not just about the money. If your intentions are good, you'll be rewarded and not just monetarily.

A "QB Darla" story:

My brand found me! When I was donating my sports activity books to kids in hospitals, I met hundreds of kids going through chemo treatments, getting bandages removed from severe burns, going through surgeries, and more. The things these kids endured broke my heart. Those families know they are forever in my heart. I was visiting Ava, a little girl who had leukemia. She was too little to understand my activity books, but she loved to sing. I asked her mom if I could bring her a karaoke machine while she was in the clinic to take her mind off her treatments, and she said yes. I'll never forget that day. I showed up with a karaoke machine, glow-in-the-dark necklaces, and my activity books. Her eyes lit up, and she began to sing her favorite songs, and for that brief moment, her pain was taken away. Her doctor came in to check on her and joined in on the fun. That same day, Braxton and Ben were getting their chemo treatments. They were old enough to follow their favorite teams and enjoy my books. One loved Alabama, and one loved Auburn, so we had fun joking about the wins and losses. They did the maze, the crosswords, and their chemo treatments blew by in a flash. Brax just graduated from high school as valedictorian, and guess where he was going to college? Yes, Roll Tide! War Eagle, Ben. I didn't care at all about my business or personal brand that day. That day was about giving those kids something to distract them and keep their minds off the chemo being pumped into their little fragile bodies. If I could've taken those needles for them, I would have. Life is about making a difference in other people's lives. It's about love and kindness. It's about hopes and dreams. It's about faith, family, and friends.

Oftentimes, we get caught up in our own personal wants and needs and forget that there are others struggling to survive, trying to make enough money to put food on the table, getting abused, dealing with the death of a loved one, or being addicted to harmful substances. Count your blessings and be mindful of those around you. Life isn't always rainbows and butterflies.

CHAPTER 2

Who is Brand YOU?

There are many ways to discover who you are and what your brand should be. Sometimes, a brand finds you, and sometimes, you find your brand. Here are a few questions you can answer to help you define your brand:

-What was your childhood like?

-Who were your mentors?

-Did you have any heroes or people you looked up to?

-What are your dreams?

-Who in your life can you surround yourself with to reach your goals?

-Are you spending time doing things you can eliminate to focus more on things that will result in your success?

-Who are the content creators who build you up that you can follow?

-Who do you find yourself continually answering to that may not align with your goals? Could you set your media to see less of them?

-What books can you read and podcasts can you listen to that will help you continually learn?

-What do you expect to accomplish from building a personal brand?

-How can you use your brand to help the universe?

Once you answer these questions, you'll be able to create a personal marketing plan.

A "QB Darla" story: It was my birthday. I had no idea how old I was turning. I just knew that I wanted to have a birthday party... a different kind of birthday party. I invited all of my friends to donate presents for me. The only requirement was that they had to be toys and gifts for kids ages 5-15 because my birthday party was going to be for the kids I had met who had illnesses and often were not invited or unable to attend birthday parties. The invites went out, and the planning began. My friends came over to help decorate, the bounce house arrived, the ice cream truck bustled in, Santa ho-ho'ed his way in, college football players joined, and the Chick-fil-A cow mooed her way in. I was more nervous for this than I was flying in the air as a cheerleader during a big Ball State rivalry game. The kids arrived, and I had a cake made for them, a swimming pool for them to jump in, and many activities.

Then, Santa and college football stars passed out their gifts. My family joined in and played basketball with the kids in the pool. The smiles I saw made this the best birthday I've ever had. No matter what kind of brand you're building, remember what your passion is and follow your heart.

BRAND ♡ YOU

YOUR PERSONALITY TRAITS	YOUR FRIENDS
YOUR HOBBIES	YOUR GIFTS

YOUR FAVORITE MENTORS	YOUR WEAKNESSES
YOUR IMPACT	YOUR LEGACY

CHAPTER 3

Create a Plan

Once you define what kind of personal brand you want, you need to write a marketing plan. Every corporation needs one. Why wouldn't you write one for yourself to define your goals and action steps to achieve them?

The best way for me to articulate how to do this is to write one for my personal brand and share that as an example. I hope this helps you understand how to write a plan, whether it's for your personal brand or for a dual corporate-led brand integrating your personal brand. I really like using the business model canvas. It is a snapshot of your marketing plan on one page in a chart format. It's great to fill that out and post it near your desk area to remain focused.

Marketing Plan

QB Darla Hall—personal brand

Witty Publications-book brand

Frontdoor-corporate brand (this example can be for any business you work for, but keep in mind there may be corporate guidelines to uphold).

Overview:

QB Darla strives to motivate others to believe in their talents and utilize their platforms to help others, share experiences, make people laugh, achieve more, believe in themselves, and love life.

Target Audience:

Adults 18+, men and women equally

Children 8-13 for activity and storybooks

Front door-my full-time job

Moxie Medical—an investment in which I own equity

Witty Solutions—my publications business for books

(For practical purposes, this example will only include my personal branding and not my corporate branding).

Platforms:

Facebook—As of January 2025, Facebook had 3.065 billion daily active users, which is more than a third of the world's population. Facebook's user base is expected to increase by 75% by 2027. The majority access it on their phone, and the average use is 7 hours a month. As of April 2024, 23% of Facebook users were aged 18–24, 31.1% were aged 25–34, and 20.2% were aged 35–44. As of January 2024,

56.8% of Facebook users identified as male, and 43.2% identified as female.

Facebook only allows you to have 5,000 friends, so once you maximize that, you'll need to ask people to follow you. I get embarrassed sometimes when people send me requests, and I have to ask them to follow me instead of connecting with me. It's either that or you must unfriend someone to add them as a friend. For people trying to build a personal brand to help others, it's hard to unfriend anyone. I think... what if that person needed to hear a message to make them smile, and I removed them? Ugh... makes my heart hurt. I've had many men reach out to me to tell me that they were depressed and thinking about suicide, but then my videos popped up, and they smiled and moved forward. They kept fighting the sadness and tried to find their way. Never underestimate the power of impact you have on these platforms. Many would never be vulnerable and tell you if you have saved their lives or made a difference. Most are silent followers. Just know that what you say and post does matter to the mental health of others.

I personally spend 60% of my efforts on Facebook and LinkedIn doing posts, reels, stories, and short motivational videos. The other 40% is divided among the rest of the platforms. On average, I spend 1 hour a week creating and posting content and 1 hour a week growing my followers. Creating content comes easy for me because I've had a lot of education, self-taught skills, and natural writing and speaking skills. You may need to spend 2-3 hours a week on content creation to get started and 1-2 hours a week to build your followers. This truly depends on the person's skill level and the amount of research needed to create good content.

I have a QB Darla page where I post motivational content, family photos, and life experiences. I have a Witty Publications page where I only talk about my kids' books. I have a real estate page where I post anything to do with my corporate brand. This helps keep everything clean for various audiences.

The best way to learn from me on social media is to follow along on all of my platforms to see what I post.

Instagram—This platform has 2 billion daily active users. 169 million of those users are in the United States. Instagram excels with users ages 16-26. Users spend an average of 16 minutes a day on Instagram. Reels account for more than half of the time spent here. The sweet spot for reels is 30-:90 in length. Any more than that, they are not as effective. 46.8M people will make a purchase from Instagram a year. It's a great place to share photos and short videos. Direct messages are effective as well.

I enjoy scrolling through stories and posting photos and stories. It's a quick and easy way to use photos, videos, and short messages to reach a younger audience.

I keep this content light-hearted and fun. I post a lot of photos, and my Facebook reels are duplicated here. I post stories at least 4 times a week to keep my audience engaged and to make someone smile.

LinkedIn—This platform boasts over 1 billion users in more than 200 countries. Most LinkedIn users are between the ages of 25 and 34 and are millennials. 56.4% of LinkedIn users are male, and 43.6% are female. LinkedIn users are more likely to have higher incomes and education levels. 65 million users search for jobs on LinkedIn each week. Over 67 million companies have profiles on LinkedIn. Over 136,000 schools have profiles on LinkedIn. Video is one of the fastest-growing formats on LinkedIn, with viewership up 36% year-over-year. LinkedIn advertising earned over $6 billion in revenue in 2022.

I personally have used LinkedIn to reel in very big fish. I like to throw my line in where the fish are biting. This platform is a great way to reach decision-makers. When I needed to find out who was making the book-buying decisions at big box retailers, I used LinkedIn Premium and messaged the bigwigs. I got a great response, but the reason was that I created a product they liked using their brand and told them how they would benefit from it. Every company wants more profits. You've got to design messaging that relates to their goals. It can't be all about you and your product. Keep your messages direct and to the point. These people are busy, and if you're lucky, they will click to open your message and give it three seconds. Those three seconds better WOW them.

QB Darla's story: I wanted to win the Ace Hardware account because I had created these adorable kids' activity books that taught kids about painting, building, and other trades. I looked up every single CEO, CFO, Product Manager, and any decision-maker I could find. I created a short message letting them know I had a product to add value and get youth to engage with their brand. Once they accepted, I sent them a sample and asked who I could set up a meeting with. Lo and behold, I got a response after three consistent months of prospecting with them. I set up a meeting, they loved it, and I was a preferred vendor within a year. My books were in the Ace Hardware stores across the country. I followed that up with Caterpillar and other national brands. LinkedIn works if you use it wisely.

I try to post on this platform at least once a week because it needs to be geared towards business people. At times, I'll post fun messages because even the most serious business professional needs to have fun. I utilize Messenger a lot when I need to connect with a specific professional. I get thousands of birthday messages, and I try to reply to each one. I've received several young professionals who have reached out to me for advice, and I allow them to call me. I believe that if you have reached some level of success in anything you do, you should pay it back to others to create a revolving goodwill locomotive. When you help someone else without anything in return, you are teaching them to do the same. It's a contagious infection of love and kindness. A good balance of staying focused on your goals and helping others is possible!

TikTok—This platform has 1.04 billion monthly active users worldwide. In the U.S., 170 million people use TikTok. TikTok's U.S. revenue reached $16 billion in 2023. U.S. adult users spend an average of 53.8 minutes per day on TikTok. In Q1 2024, TikTok was downloaded 137 million times.

According to TikTok CEO's (Shou Chew) statement in January 2024, TikTok has 170 million monthly active users in the U.S.. Globally, the average time spent on TikTok was 95 minutes per day, more than on any other social network. In the U.S., users spend an average of 53.8 minutes per day on TikTok, eMarketer analysis shows. More than half (55%) of TikTok weekly active users in the U.S. are between 18 and 34 years old. Only 14% of TikTok weekly users are 55 years old and older.

I love to dance, so I enjoy watching the dance trends on this platform. I also participate in some of them. I don't have time to learn the hard dances, so I lean into the easy trends. They are fun to watch and learn from. Occasionally, I'll post them to my other social networks to show my personality. It takes me back to my cheerleading days. I also love to discover new talent. As you scroll through, you see that there are some extremely talented artists who haven't made it big yet. I love cheering for the underdog.

Grassroots—There are many tactics you can pursue in your communities and abroad. Here are a few ideas:

-Join clubs or groups that interest you, church or faith-based communities.

-Attend events—Chamber of Commerce, associations, clubs, networking groups, workshops, fundraisers.

-Seek board positions—this gives you credibility and helps you with connections. Typically, boards allow you to be passionate about a cause or something that interests you.

I am a social butterfly, but I also enjoy my quiet time, and I get 8 hours of sleep most nights. I attend a fair amount of events and community functions, I create content daily, and I work very hard every day. Every day that I wake up, I ask myself a rhetorical question: What can you do today that will help someone else have a great day? I try to answer that with actions. I created content to post or give compliments when I'm out in public.

Friends/Family—Friends and family can help you grow your personal brands if they understand your goals. Keep in mind that not all of them will support you. There are many factors surrounding this, and not all families are the same. There may be jealousy to contend with, or they may just not want to get involved. It's OK. You can still love them and respect them.

I love my family. My three sons come first because I love them so much, and I try to teach them good values. I'm perfectly imperfect, and I share my struggles with them as well. They follow me and enjoy my positivity. I see them looking out for others, and it makes me so proud. It's so important to have a reason behind your personal brand, and they are my everything.

Traditional Media—There is paid media such as Facebook ads, radio spots, TV ads, digital marketing, billboards, and magazines. That, of course, takes money.

If you have a lot of money, paid media is a viable method of marketing. Television ads, radio ads, magazine ads, direct mail, social media paid ads, and billboards are a few of these options. Social media ads are less expensive and can be very targeted.

Beware of letting someone else run your social media. There is power in keeping your content authentic, engaging with your audience, and not being robotic. People can see right through. I personally don't use paid advertising, but I'm not opposed to it. If you have a small budget, test it before you spend a lot of money.

Public Relations—There are public relations opportunities where you can be a guest on morning talk shows and guests on podcasts. You can create press releases to send to news outlets if you have something newsworthy to share or if you are an expert on a subject they are interested in. You can even create your own podcast and YouTube shows. You can write books to establish yourself as an expert in your field.

I love writing and sharing my knowledge with others. I enjoy sharing my mistakes so that others can learn from them. Sometimes, vulnerability makes a person more relatable. I'll share a few stories later about this.

Goals:

-Increase followers by 10% each year

-Gain followers who engage with my content

-Create specific content for each platform based on its strengths

-Incorporate my brand into my corporate brand to help them succeed

-Continue educating myself on motivational messages that help people

-Add value to people's lives

-Utilize my personal brand to build relationships with realtors to help my corporate brand

-Establish myself as an expert in areas of marketing, branding, relationship building, sales, and helping others

-Incorporate my personal brand with my Witty Publications book business

-Utilize the power of my personal brand to build relationships within my corporate job

Strategies/Tactics:

-Consistent posts-2-3 posts per week, 1-2 videos per week

-Publish one motivational book per year

-Watch one video/ a podcast per week and read one book per quarter that helps me grow as a person or in business

-Create more posts that add value to people's lives or business

-Set up workshops, Zooms, and events for my clients

-Make videos using my personality and branding knowledge for my clients

-Continue creating kids' and adults' books

-Build my personal brand into my corporate brand through sales meetings, training, marketing, and communications

Competition:

-Authors, speakers, and content creators on all platforms who are vying for attention to their content

-Competitive companies bring to my clients' attention

-Negativity

Budget:

This can cost $0 if you use social media and all free platforms.

You may also want to come up with a reasonable budget once you get ready to grow your level of impact.

Low-end budget example:

-$5,000 publishing book launch

-$2,000 marketing materials

-$3,000 misc materials to support paid ads

High-end budget example:

-$30,000 hire a professional company to guide you and help you with your content, brand strategy, and implementation

-$20,000 marketing materials and advertising

-$10,000 book creation, working with a ghostwriter, marketing, and distribution

Your budget will depend on your financial situation. If you have no money in your savings, the good news is that you can still build your platform and create content. You can still get followers and impact people's lives. You can still begin the process of building your brand. There are many benefits to securing a job with a company that offers a 401K and health benefits. As you are building your brand, don't lose sight of how to build your wealth and savings. A budget for your personal brand shouldn't be spent if you don't have it to spend. There are many tools, podcasts, and resources for building a solid financial foundation. This is always important to meet your basic needs.

In conclusion, your marketing plan doesn't need to be a 30-page document. Keep it basic so you can execute it each year. It is a working document and can change daily.

The most important takeaway is to DO IT. Write the plan. Visualize the results. Make it happen!

Take ACTION!

Aim high

Challenge yourself

Take risks

Ignite the fuel within your soul

Own your mistakes

Never give up

A "QB Darla" story: I was deep in my sports activity book business. It was a whirlwind. One day, I was creating a product from scratch for a little boy's gift, then the next, I was flying to Vegas on a wing and a prayer to seek an investor to grow my book business so I could continue doing good with it. Coach Saban and several other coaches were using my books to donate to kids in hospitals, and I was grinding it out. I was cold-calling and getting orders from many college bookstores, Cracker Barrel, Sam's Club, Costco, and many more. I had publishing deals with Ingram and had them on Amazon. I competed in a venture capital contest and won $15,000, which allowed me to add more titles and keep going. It was hard work, but I'd see the smiles on the kids' faces in chemo, and I'd keep fighting another day. Any entrepreneur can attest that building anything from scratch is a lot of blood, sweat, and tears. Mostly sweat. I had a $17,000 CLC licensing invoice coming due at any moment. This would make or break my business. I remember lying on my couch in tears, knowing this would be the end. Then, I got a Facebook message from Gideon's grandma saying how thankful she was because he loved my prayer activity book.

Gideon was a little boy who was a miracle story. His parents nearly lost him during a brain surgery he had to undergo to help with his seizures. He loved Tennessee football, so I gave him a Smokey activity book. I had a Navy SEAL friend of mine visit him in the hospital, and he gave him cool helicopters and Navy playsets. I brought bubbles and whatever I could afford at the time. I developed a special relationship with him over several years. I hit a home run with him on a Miracle Field, and we became buddies.

A few months earlier, I had received a large order from a big retailer who said my books would be put out through the holidays. They didn't uphold that, and I felt betrayed. Most people at this point would've given up and shut down their business. I didn't. I fought. I called the CEO every single day for two straight weeks. I was determined to make sure they understood that not only were they messing with me, but they were impacting these kids to whom I was donating books. My momma bear instincts were in full force. I finally got a callback. The CEO said, "Miss, I've gotten every message. Do you realize this is borderline harassment?"

I said, "Sir, thank you for calling. I was told my books would be out until Christmas, and they not only pulled them off the shelves, but they put stickers on them and tried to return them. They also didn't put them out in some locations. I create these books for a bigger purpose than just making money. I create them to help children in hospitals, so I'd appreciate it if you'd re-evaluate this decision."

He graciously said, "I'll get with my team."

I didn't hear back from him.

Fast forward a few months, and that bill was due. I walked out to my mailbox, not expecting anything that day other than junk mail. Holy moly! Guacamole! Me, oh my! I saw an envelope from this big retailer, and my first thought was that they were billing me for something that I wouldn't be able to pay. No! You won't believe this! I was shocked! I received a check for $17,350... a few pennies more than I owed. Wow! I ran around my house with happy tears because I knew how hard I had fought this battle. I knew that I loved to fight another day for my family, my business, my investors, and these amazing kiddos. Never give up on your dreams! Keep fighting the good fight.

For more inspiration and branding insights, connect with QB Darla on social media. Just scan the QR code to follow along!

CHAPTER 4

How to Build Brand YOU

Many focus on content, but they have no idea how to build their number of followers. If you don't have followers, your content won't be seen. I believe that it's just as important to build your following at the same time you are creating content. You can always repurpose your content that isn't seen by many once you get a bigger audience.

How do you build your following?

-Attend events. Show up at as many networking and social events as you can. Ask people to follow you to stay in touch. Instead of handing out business cards or flyers, I'll say, "Follow me on Facebook or LinkedIn to stay in touch." I have them find me right there and add me. There's no better time than the present! If they walk away without following you right then, they will likely forget you existed.

-Post consistently. The amount depends on each unique person. Just keep in front of your audience.

-Post in a variety of ways. Stories, posts, live videos, photos, DM's, events, etc., maximize the number of views by varying your types of posts.

-Add Value. Always think of the end-user. Why will they watch you? Why should they care?

-Engage. Respond to your followers. Ask questions. Create polls. Respond to their posts. Write helpful articles. Post great books to read and anything that will interest your followers. Offer advice and use your network to connect with people.

-Lead or become an expert. Set the trends. If you don't drink, be proud of it and make it a popular trend. If you like a brand of sunglasses, own the vibe and promote them as if they were already best sellers. Lead your followers down a positive path of growth and positivity. Help solve problems.

-Create networking events. At these events, ask for follow.

-Use hashtags that have high engagement

-Ask the experts. Attend workshops. I don't have all of the answers, but if I need to know something, I'll read a book or find a workshop to soak in the knowledge I'm missing.

A "QB Darla" story: One important thing to keep in mind as you are building your followers is to get the right kind of followers. You want people who support your overall mission. I've always stayed authentic and written my own content, filmed my own videos, and never got caught up in doing things professionally. A perfect example of this is when I was creating a motivational video at the Vestavia Hills Country Club in Alabama. I searched for the perfect location to encourage people to "be a light" to others. I found a gorgeous mountaintop view that I was sure was just the most magical spot that people would enjoy. I nestled down on a rock with a red brush under my feet. I propped my camera up in just the right position and started recording. I messed up, so I had to start over. All of a sudden, I felt something stinging my feet... then my legs. It felt like something was biting me. Yikes! I looked down to find hundreds of fire ants biting me. I screamed, quickly ran off, and tried to brush them off me as quickly as possible. I was left with red welts all over me. Did I post that video? Yes! Why? Because it was me. It was a perfect example of how imperfect I am and how it's OK to laugh at yourself sometimes. Life is serious all the time. Let's all take a deep breath and realize that the content we share isn't always going to be perfect. Share the flaws. Share the mishaps. Share real life. Life is too short to fake it. Let your hair down and live a little. "Be a light... ant bites and all!"

CHAPTER 5

How to Stay Focused & Humble While Building Brand YOU

You are not invincible. Pain will come. Hurt will happen. Death is real. Heartbreak sucks. You will get distracted from your goals. It's OK to grieve, but please try to heal and get back in the groove. I know... easier said than done sometimes. Your other loved ones and this world need you. You owe it to yourself to be a fighter. If you step into the ring and get knocked down, it's up to you to dig deep to get back up and go another round.

When creating content, try not to get too caught up in how many likes every single post gets. Think about how much value you have provided to others. Did you make someone smile? Did you offer helpful tips? Did you help someone get better at their craft? Did you provide good business advice? Did you think about your audience instead of yourself?

There are many distractions that get you off the path. It's easy to get deterred. How many emails do you get in a given day? Here are a few tips to stay focused:

-Unsubscribe from the spam and junk emails.

-Limit time to scroll social media to 15 minutes per day, at a time when you aren't working or selling.

-Set your notifications on your phone to silent during selling times. Designate certain hours for strict selling times.

-Put a sign on your office door so you aren't disturbed during primary selling hours.

-Plan times to go on vacation or disconnect so you aren't disturbed during refresh and fired up about your productivity.

-Crank up your favorite tunes and get revved up about your performance goals.

-Envision the end game. If you're working hard to save money for a boat, then pick out your boat and go test drive it.

-Change up your routines. If, on a given day, you wake up, drink your coffee, and drive to work taking the same route, try taking a scenic route where you can see the countryside.

-Exercise and try a healthier diet.

A "QB Darla" story: This will be an emotional one because when I think of humility, I think of two different stories in my life. The first one is a little boy named Ryan. He loved his favorite team, and I was able to take him to a championship game. He told his mom that it was the best day of his life. We threw a birthday party for him because he had brain cancer, and we weren't sure how much time he had left on earth. He got so many presents that he wanted to give some of his gifts to the other kids at the hospital. These kids, going through struggles that we will never comprehend, are humble, kind, and selfless. They are amazing!

Another story about humility happened when I was speaking in Dallas at a convention. On my way to that engagement, I met an Uber driver named Clarence. He was a preacher and very proud to be driving me around. After chatting with him from the back seat for a while, I knew he was special. I felt his vibe. I asked him to pull over so I could get in the front seat. I asked about something that reminded him of his son.

He proceeded to tell me a story about how his son died, and he was driving around one day and saw a homeless man. He pulled over to ask the man what he needed. The man looked down at his bare feet and said, "All I need is a pair of shoes to put on my feet."

Clarence said he sat there for a few minutes and pondered this, knowing the shoes he had on his feet had belonged to his late son, who had passed away recently. Clarence took those shoes off and gave them to the man. Clarence then shared with me that those shoes were one of the only possessions he had left of his son, but that his son lived in his heart, and that man needed those shoes that day. Wow! Talk about humility. Clarence was humble and gracious and shared the love of God. I went on to speak to 200 people and shared that story with them. If you ever go to Dallas and get to ride with

Clarence, know that he'll also give you the shirt off his back if you need it. As you are building your platforms, be humble and kind. You never know who is watching you.

CHAPTER 6

How to Do Good Being Brand YOU

I would like to challenge all influencers, leaders, bosses, and anyone with a social media account to consider the following ideas to impact the world in a positive way:

1- Use your platforms to do something good. If you are a savvy businessman/woman, use it to offer advice to others trying to set up a new business. If you are a teacher, use it to help other teachers. If you are an electrician, offer advice to homeowners. You get the idea. Add value. Pay it forward.

2- Stay positive because you never know who is watching you and trying to be more like you. You never know if someone is having a bad day and needs something to smile about. You may never know how powerful your content is or what it means to those who follow you. There are enough negative people in the world. Why would we ever want to jump in on that to tear anyone down or make people feel sad, lonely, unimportant, or humiliated? Life is too short.

3- Refrain from oversharing sensitive subjects. Save those conversations for in-person, not social platforms. Let's commit to helping others, positive messaging, and any content that will make the world a better place.

4- Prioritize doing good on top of making money. Yes, you need to make a living. Many companies need great people. It's healthy to work a job that teaches accountability, hard work, discipline, building relationships, selling, and motivation. It's great if you can make extra income being an influencer or selling goods on platforms, but remember that you only have one life to live. Whatever you do and however you choose to make a living, include something that helps someone every day. Add value to other people's lives. Be a good role model for our future generations. Live a healthy, balanced life. Go out there a make a million dollars! If you do, try to give back to others, whether that be monetarily, sound advice, kindness, or time.

Ask yourself these questions:

1-How do you want people to remember you?

2-What do you want your legacy to be?

A "QB Darla" story: I've had many people tell me how much I've changed their lives, and that is heavy to even think about. One evening, I got a phone call from a man who followed me on LinkedIn. He said, "QB Darla, I was afraid to call you, but I wanted to tell you how much your posts mean to me. I was going through a lot of health issues, feeling depressed about life, and not in a good place. I browsed through my LinkedIn feed, and there you were, bright and cheerful, reminding me that I could overcome hard times. I couldn't help but stop and watch your video because you are bubbly and always smiling. You saved me, and I just wanted to let you know how much I appreciate that."

I was extremely touched and felt honored that my positivity helped him when he needed it the most. I'm still connected to that young man today, and I'm proud to say he has graduated from college and is well on his way to his version of success. It motivated me to keep posting content even if it helped one or two people a day. The purpose of my content was to help those who might be too afraid to reach out but are still watching, listening, thinking, and choosing to live their best lives.

CHAPTER 7

How to Lead Using Brand YOU

A leader possesses certain qualities or learns to lead by watching others and educating themselves on how to lead. If you are a born leader, great! If you had to learn to lead, great! Leaders step up to the plate when they are needed, and the good ones want their people to succeed.

What makes a good leader?

-Confidence

-Selflessness

-Dedication

-Resilience

-Intelligence

If you have a social media presence at all, you are a leader, whether you intend to be or not. If you have 10 followers, you never know how vulnerable those 10 people are. Is your content hurting or helping those 10 humans?

Social media is a free platform where anyone is able to express their thought and views. With this opportunity comes great responsibility. We owe it to others to use it for good, not evil. If we have good intentions of making others feel good about themselves, then we create a safe environment. If we post mean things to hurt others, it becomes unsafe.

A "QB Darla" story: This is a story about a boy who didn't know he was a leader in his community. His name was Reese. He was living his best teenage years, going to football games, prom, church, and events. I met Reese and his family through my activity books and followed his journey throughout his life on social media. Reese had a terminal heart condition and wasn't expected to live nearly as long as he did. He loved playing sports, and his dream was to coach football. He made it clear that God was his leader. Reese unintentionally became a role model by sharing his story openly and honestly. He passed away, and many attended his funeral. Reese may never know just how big of a leader he was to his community. His legacy will live on forever. His light will continue to shine on those who followed his journey close and from afar. A person may never know the impact they are making. You better believe that people are watching, listening, and learning from the content you are posting. Use the power of influence for good, not evil.

CHAPTER 8

How to Monetize Brand YOU

I personally am not an expert in monetizing your personal brand, so I used ChatGPT to weigh in on this subject matter. My personal brand is focused on helping others succeed, so the money isn't my highest priority. I realize that I need to learn more about monetization and make money so that I have the resources to empower and help inspire the world. I need money to get my children's book business going again, so I can help children in hospitals by donating more books.

Personally, I monetize my brand in two ways: 1- I write books for adults and children. I'm hopeful someday to re-establish myself as the creator of storybooks and activity books for children, plus continue motivational content and public speaking for adults. 2- Public speaking. I do workshops and motivational speaking. Public speaking isn't for the weak. It takes guts to share your journey with hundreds on a stage with a microphone. Self-doubt creeps in, and you ask yourself... is my message going to resonate and inspire others? Is it going to relate to them? Are they going to take a nap or wander off into space because it is too boring? It feels like getting on a frightening roller coaster, plummeting down a four-story hill as your stomach sinks in just before running out to the stage. You can either get sick or suck it up and know that there is a chance you could really make a difference in someone's life. It's frightening, yet rewarding.

Artificial intelligence can be a helpful resource as long as it doesn't remove the authenticity and creative input from the human heart. Transparency is critical in order to be honest and transparent. Authors, songwriters, speakers, and influencers need to use it, but use it with caution. It can create thought starters, but don't allow it to write what you want to express. It can fill voids where you are weak, but it cannot replace your lifelong lessons and soulful expression of truths. It can help, but it should not do the work for you. People are paying good money for honesty and truth. You might be able to mislead some, but will you be able to sleep well at night if you aren't truthful? There is nothing that can replace the human heart and soul.

Chaptgpt's input when I asked for help teaching others about monetizing their personal brands:

You've built the foundation—your name is known, your voice is distinct, and your audience is listening. Now comes the part many people dream about: turning your personal brand into a sustainable source of income. Monetizing your personal brand isn't just about slapping your name on a product or launching a paid course. It's about aligning your unique value with the needs of your audience and offering solutions they're willing to pay for.

In this chapter, we will break down the steps to start earning from your personal brand, explore different revenue streams, and dive into real-world strategies that help you turn influence into income.

1. Define Your Value Proposition

Before you can monetize, you must be crystal clear on what makes you valuable. Ask yourself:

·   What problem do I solve?

·   Who do I help?

·   Why would someone pay me instead of someone else?

Your value proposition is the bridge between your personal story and your audience's needs. For example, if you're a fitness influencer, your value might not just be workouts—it could be helping busy moms feel confident in 30 minutes a day. That specificity matters.

2. Know Your Audience

You can't sell to everyone, and you shouldn't try. Knowing your audience means understanding:

· What they struggle with

· What they're already paying for

· What content or products do they respond to

Use analytics, polls, DMs, and comments to gather insights. When you know what your audience values, you can create offerings they want, not just what you think they need.

3. Choose Your Revenue Streams

There are several proven ways to monetize a personal brand. Here are the most effective:

a) Digital Products

· Ebooks, guides, templates, and courses are low-cost to produce and high-margin.

· Great if you have specialized knowledge (marketing, mindset, design, etc.)

b) Coaching & Consulting

· Ideal for service-based personal brands (e.g., life coaches, career advisors).

· One-on-one or group formats.

c) Affiliate Marketing

·   Promote products you love and earn a commission.

·   Works well if you have a loyal, engaged audience and trust is high.

d) Sponsored Content & Brand Deals

·   Partner with companies that align with your niche.

·   Focus on authentic collaborations—your audience can smell a cash grab from a mile away.

e) Memberships & Subscriptions

·   Platforms like Patreon or exclusive communities (Discord, Facebook Groups).

·   Offer exclusive content, access, or Q&A sessions.

f) Merchandise & Physical Products

·   T-shirts, planners, supplements, or any branded physical product.

·   Be cautious with upfront costs and inventory.

g) Speaking Engagements & Events

·   Get paid to speak at conferences, podcasts, or panels.

·   Hosting your own events (virtual or in-person) can also be profitable.

4. Build Trust Before Selling

People don't buy from people they don't trust. Focus on serving your audience before you ever ask them to open their wallets.

- Share free value consistently.
- Show results—yours or your clients.
- Be authentic, transparent, and relatable.

A great rule of thumb: for every "ask" you make (sale, promotion), deliver five pieces of value-packed content.

5. Create a Clear Customer Journey

Your audience needs to know what the next step is.

- Are they moving from free content to a $9 ebook?
- From a free webinar to a $997 course?
- From Instagram posts to a monthly membership?

Design a "value ladder" where each level builds trust and leads to higher-value offers.

6. Package and Price with Confidence

Your offer needs to be easy to understand, visually appealing, and perceived as valuable.

- Name it with intention (don't just say "coaching call"—say "90-Minute Brand Breakthrough Session").

- Price it based on transformation, not time.

- Don't be afraid to charge what you're worth—underpricing signals inexperience or lack of confidence

7. Promote Like a Pro

You don't need to be "salesy" to sell. Focus on storytelling, results, and testimonials.

- Use social proof: "Here's what happened after Sarah took my course…"

- Use urgency and scarcity: "Only 10 spots left" or "Enrollment closes Friday."

- Show behind the scenes: let your audience feel part of the journey.

Marketing is just sharing your solution with the people who need it.

8. Diversify Over Time

Start with one or two monetization strategies. Once they're profitable, reinvest in others. Many six- and seven-figure personal brands have 3–5 active revenue streams working in harmony.

The key: start lean, validate your offer, then scale smart.

Monetizing your personal brand isn't about chasing trends or quick cash grabs—it's about building real value for real people. Your brand is your reputation. When you treat it like a business, stay consistent, and prioritize trust, income becomes a natural byproduct of the impact you're already making.

Your audience is ready. The question is—are you?

I'd like to encourage you to create content to help people, first and foremost. If you make money, that is great if it is helping your family put food on the table. Stay focused on creating content that is helpful to others, and you will help future generations realize the positive power of influence.

CHAPTER 9

How to Utilize Brand YOU to Get a Job and In Your Job

You are a walking billboard to those around you. When you see a billboard of two fit individuals using a treadmill to exercise, you may stare at the advertisement for many different reasons. 1- They are pretty. 2- You want to look like them. 3- You may want to buy a treadmill. 4- You may or may not even see who the retailer is that sells the treadmill. Big brands spend big bucks to get your attention through emotions and recall. They try to appeal to your senses of sight, smell, touch, or feeling. They try to reach you using various mediums to ensure that you can recall the brand so you will purchase theirs instead of a competitor's.

This same advertising philosophy holds true to building your personal brand. You are the brand. What you say and do reflects how people perceive you. As a walking billboard, the choices you make are import, the people you associate yourself with matter, and how you treat people counts. Your physical appearance and what you wear may impact your brand.

If you think for one second that you are not important enough to worry about your personal brand, that's not true. No matter if you have 0 followers or 20,000 followers on social media, you still likely have people who look up to you. If you think you don't know enough people or you have not accomplished enough yet, please remember that even if one person looks up to you, you are worthy. If you think you're not physically attractive enough to influence others, that's not accurate. If you think you are not famous enough, it doesn't matter. I'd ask you... What's your definition of fame? Fame is in the eye of the beholder. Success can be defined in many ways. Riches do not determine happiness. Each person has gifts and a story to share to help others. And guess what... God designed you to be exactly the way you are. You are important, you have a brand, and your journey does matter.

When you apply for jobs, you want to put your best foot forward. You need to impress the decision-maker and stand out from the other applicants.

First, you look for jobs that you feel you are qualified for. I'd like to challenge you to also apply for jobs that you aren't quite as qualified for, because everyone tends to sell themselves short. After all, you can learn as you go. Many times, we need to dream bigger and strive for more than we think we can achieve. Our minds often convince us that we aren't good enough, strong enough, pretty enough, or resourceful enough. Be careful not to allow your own thoughts about yourself to stop you from accomplishing more than what you think you can do. I'd make a bet that there are people around you who believe that you are capable of greater things than you could even imagine for yourself.

Next, you prepare your resume. You list your qualifications and experience that relate closest to what their job description is. Oh boy! This is terrifying when you first start out because you have no experience with anything other than going to school. You are relying on someone to take a chance on you with zero knowledge of anything related to the job. You doubt yourself. You might even decide not to apply for it because it might hurt to get rejected.

Oh boy! Let's talk about rejection. If I had a quarter for every time I was rejected in a relationship, a job, a business, or as a writer, I'd be a millionaire. Rejection is part of life. It makes us stronger if we let it. It builds character because it reminds us that we need to learn more. We can't let rejection define us. We've got to let it fuel the fire within us.

Apply for that job that you think you can't get. You might surprise yourself, and when you land it, you'll be even more motivated to learn the skills and prove them right for taking a chance on you. Now, wouldn't that be fun?

During the application process, you're well on your way to building your personal brand. In doing so, you may be unknowingly thinking about how your skills and gifts may impact others in business and in life. Your name may not be up in lights yet in Hollywood (and to be honest, I'm not sure that's a good goal), but your personal brand is getting ready to make a difference in people's lives.

"QB Darla Story:" I was working at Ball State Sports Information office and applied for my first real job at the Amateur Athletic Union. I had written a few press releases, created some entry-level designs for the teams, and could mess up a mean football stat and give the wrong tackle to the five players who piled on top of each other. I saw a position for Assistant Director of Public Relations for the AAU. It sounded cool, but I had no real experience other than that I loved sports. I doubted whether I should even apply. Then, my positive mindset kicked in, and I said to myself, "What do I have to lose to apply?"

The only thing that would happen is that I wouldn't get an interview and would have to face rejection. I've been there and done that with relationships and sports. So, I applied with no fear of rejection! I didn't get a call for a while, so I anxiously awaited. My boss at BSU laughed at me and said, "I gave a reference for you today, but the guy said you forgot to put your phone number on your resume. I gave it to him, so you can expect a call unless he calls someone who didn't forget such an important detail."

I was so embarrassed but grateful that he tracked me down. I got the job! Now what? I had no idea what I was doing. I had a great attitude and a will to learn and do whatever it took to go above and beyond. I won Employee of the Year after a few years of dedication and hard work. I was off to the races! You can be, too, if you don't allow fear of rejection to impact your decisions.

CHAPTER 10

Brand YOU for Realtors

Realtors have two brands: your broker brand and your personal brand, Brand YOU. Your broker brand is traditionally the brand that your broker prefers the consumers to see first. That large logo that you see on the yard sign. Sometimes, they will allow you to put your brand alongside theirs by following their brand guidelines. It's important to respect those wishes and create a positive relationship with them. They are providing you with the tools and resources necessary to be successful in the industry.

Don't be afraid to push the envelope. Ask if you can add your photo and personal brand to everything you do. Figure out a good solution that works well for both parties.

Challenge yourself to create a personal branding plan combined with your brokerage brand. Write a plan and execute it.

Show up! Go into the office to make your calls, set up your CRM, create your content, learn from your peers, and attend sales meetings.

Learn constantly. The market shifts, rates change, innovative tools are created, new competition surfaces, and vendors change. When those things happen, you want to be the first to know so you can become the expert in all things real estate.

Allow yourself to showcase your personality in your brand and be authentic. Follow other realtors to learn from their content. Some agents are funny. Some are strictly business. Every single agent will be unique. You've got a gift. You've got a rare personality that should shine in the industry. Use your skills, education, leadership, and personality to guide your brand.

Look for learning opportunities outside of the office that enhance your personal branding. The brokerage will teach you everything you need to know about contracts, agreements, legal to-dos, data, marketing, and much more! You need to teach yourself how to define, grow, and showcase your personal brand. There are experts in this field whom you can follow. You can also watch podcasts, read books, and attend events.

Create shop talk! Identify all of the coffee shops in your community. Put a sticker or sign at your table saying, "Ask me about real estate or ask me about real estate, and I'll buy you a coffee." This may stimulate a friendly conversation and be the start of many conversations with people in your neighborhood.

Create a marketing plan for your personal brand and your corporate brand. Your buyer/seller presentations should reflect this powerful branding. Define what makes you stand apart from other realtors. Then, take action every single day to build your platforms, reach your target audiences, and build sustainable relationships.

CHAPTER 11

Brand YOU for Influencers

An influencer is a person who has the power to affect the purchasing decisions or opinions of others because of their authority, knowledge, position, or relationship with their audience, especially on social media platforms. Influencers often build trust and a following in a specific niche, such as fashion, fitness, gaming, or technology, and collaborate with brands to promote products or ideas.

An influencer is also a person in your community who has a good following and utilizes their talents to help others succeed.

No matter what type of influencer you are, it's important to utilize your platforms to encourage and uplift others.

Here are practical tips for influencers to grow their followers organically and sustainably:

Know Your Niche: Focus on a specific topic or industry (e.g., travel, beauty, tech) and stick to it. This helps attract a targeted audience.

Be Consistent: Post regularly and at optimal times. Use a content calendar to stay organized.

Create High-Quality Content: Use good lighting, clear audio, and editing tools to make your content visually appealing and professional.

Engage With Your Audience: Respond to comments and messages, ask questions, and use polls or stories to interact.

Use Hashtags Strategically: Mix popular and niche-specific hashtags to increase discoverability.

Collaborate With Others: Partner with other influencers or brands to reach new audiences.

Tell Your Story: Be authentic and relatable. Share behind-the-scenes content and personal experiences to build trust.

Leverage Trends: Participate in viral challenges or trending topics—just make sure they align with your brand.

Cross-Promote on Other Platforms: Promote your content on different social media platforms and link them together.

Analyze and Adapt: Use analytics tools to track what works and adjust your strategy accordingly.

CHAPTER 12

Brand YOU for Parents

The moment you have a child, you become a parent. You also become someone your child looks up to for advice, encouragement, and love. You have an influence on your children. They are watching you even when you think they aren't. They are listening, even when you think they aren't. Parents are not perfect. They are oftentimes still learning life lessons as they are expected to raise a child. Parenting is such a blessing and a big responsibility.

What does your parenting personal brand look like? It is whatever you paint it to be. Has your child ever brought home a drawing of your family or what they would like to be when they grow up? When their teacher asks that, they draw what they have seen and the only thing they know. Sometimes, they draw what they see in cartoons or on their devices. You might see that and quickly device that you need to work on your personal branding so your children have a positive role model to learn from.

You have a clean slate to build the brand of who you are as a parent to your children. While it's not a brand that you monetize, it might be the most important reason to build a personal brand.

As the children grow older, your brand will change.

A "QB Darla Story:" When I became a parent, I flew by the seat of my pants. I was a Ball State cheerleader who kept cheering until I couldn't fit into my skirt anymore. I didn't know what personal branding was; I had never thought about being a role model, and I certainly didn't have a clue about raising a baby. I did know that I needed to finish my degree so my kids would see me work hard to provide for them. Once my son was born, I immediately became a nurturer at times and a lion at times, ready to protect my baby cub at any cost. As they grew up, I became their teacher, coach, therapist, doctor, planner, provider, and a million other things.

One day, my youngest son was in high school, and he called me and said, "Mom, I forgot my basketball shorts, can you please bring them to school?" That day I had 3 meetings and was very busy, but I said, "Yes, of course."

I decided to go through a car wash quickly in my five minutes to spare before my meeting. I was juggling a hundred things in my mind. I saw that my sunroof was cracked open mid-wash. I went to close it and accidentally pushed the button the wrong way. Needless to say, my business suit was soaked, my hair was drenched, and I looked like a drowned rat. I'm sure when I pulled out, the guys working there had a good laugh. I just laughed at myself, went home to change, dropped off the shorts, and went to my meeting.

Parents can juggle a lot. Just remember to laugh and enjoy the challenge!

CHAPTER 13

Brand YOU for Entrepreneurs & Business Owners

In the ever-evolving world of business, one truth remains constant: people do business with people they know, like, and trust. While your products, services, or business model may be exceptional, what often makes the difference in a competitive market is you—your story, your voice, and your personal brand.

Trust and Credibility

In a crowded market, trust is currency. Customers who see a consistent and authentic personal brand are more likely to believe in your business. By demonstrating thought leadership, transparency, and values through your brand, you build credibility that sets you apart from faceless competitors.

Differentiation

What makes you different from the next business owner in your field? Your experiences, perspectives, and personality are uniquely yours. Personal branding helps you showcase those differences in a compelling way, making it easier for potential clients and partners to remember and choose you.

Visibility and Reach

With the rise of social media, podcasts, and digital media, business owners now have unprecedented access to audiences. A strong personal brand helps you amplify your message and attract opportunities—speaking engagements, partnerships, media features—that would otherwise be out of reach.

Connection with Your Audience

People crave authenticity. When you show up as a real person, not just a CEO or founder, you invite your audience to connect with you emotionally. Whether you're sharing lessons learned, behind-the-scenes glimpses of your journey, or your vision for the future, personal stories make your business more relatable and human.

When you own your own business, your guests pay attention to service, quality of product, location, cleanliness, employee interaction, and many other factors. Oftentimes, they want to know who the owner is. They want to know who they are supporting with their hard-earned dollars. This is where your personal branding comes into play. They may look at your social media to get more information about you. When you decide to own a business, your privacy may be more open to public observation.

It's important to set up company pages that are different than your personal pages. Keep in mind that your personal pages may be viewed even if you set up corporate accounts. Your personal brand may impact your corporate brand, and your corporate brand makes an impact on your personal brand.

CHAPTER 14

Pitfalls to Avoid

1- Brand YOU is not really about you. That's worth repeating... Brand YOU is NOT about YOU! It's about what you do for others. It's about how you build a brand to help others around you succeed. It's about using your skills and talents to improve the world. It's about using your brand to sell more, make more money, and do good around you.

2- Brand YOU is NOT about you creating content to get more likes, more followers, or more validation. It's not about using your talents to show off or find a mate. It's not about fame and fortune. If you're building a brand to gain instant fame, your heart is not in the right place. Check your ego at the door so you can open your heart to the things that matter most in life. You only have one chance and an average of 80 years to live life to the fullest. Let's not waste it on creating content for the wrong reasons.

3- Keep your circle the size you want it, but make sure the people in it want you to succeed. Keep a close eye out for the people you hang around because oftentimes, they influence you instead of you influencing them. Be the trendsetter and make healthy choices. Be the leader of the pack. Be the one who doesn't spread rumors or gossip. Be strong and bold in your decisions. Own who you are. Respect people who have different opinions.

4- Brand YOU is exactly that:

-You are one of a kind

-Only you can be you

-Uniquely made for a purpose

Don't allow fear to stop you. Don't allow fear of making mistakes to stop you from creating a life that is different from others. If you stop comparing yourself to celebrities and rich people, you'll learn to be confident in who you were made to be. God made each of us with our own unique fingerprints. There is a one in a billion chance you have the same fingerprint as someone else. Be proud of how you were made, with flaws and all.

5- You will make mistakes in life. We all do. It's important to learn, listen, and use those mistakes to be a better person. Mistakes often lead to more mistakes unless the first mistake isn't thought through. Why did I make that mistake? What caused it? What was the impact? Who did it hurt? What are ways I can be better? How can I learn from it? How can I use that mistake to help others avoid making the same one?

Some of the most prominent brands make mistakes. Those brands that overcame them are the ones that come out stronger in the end because they have learned what not to do and owned up to their mistake.

Forgive yourself. If you've truly learned from what you did wrong and done everything you can to improve because of it, let it go! Turn the page. Start fresh and let bygones be bygones.

CHAPTER 15

Brand YOU Becomes Your Legacy

What do you want your legacy to be? How do you want people to remember you? Everyone is different in thinking about death. Some fear it. Some look forward to it. Some talk about it. Some are cringing just reading about it. This chapter isn't going to be doom and gloom. It will give you a fresh approach to thinking about your legacy.

You work so hard 365 days a year being YOU. Incredible, unique, and amazing YOU. Imperfect, flawed, and vulnerable YOU. You have a routine. The average person gets up, showers (hopefully), drinks their coffee or tea, reads the news, goes to work, eats lunch, comes home, kisses their mate or pet, eats dinner, engages in a hobby, and then goes to bed. I'm sure there are many variations each day in each person's daily routines.

I'd like to challenge you to think about your legacy and alter your routine now based on what you determine are the most important people and lessons you'd like to leave behind for generations to come. Use these four D's to help guide your new plan.

1-Define your passion.

2-Determine what is most important.

3-Define aspirations for future generations.

4- Do more of the things that bring you joy and less of the things that don't.

Be better than average. Be extraordinary.

A "QB Darla" story: This is the story about the parents of two little boys, Hunter and Micah. Hunter was diagnosed with terminal brain cancer at the age of 7. His parents were devastated at the news. They loved both of their sons very much. I asked permission to raise money for them at my book launch, and his parents were grateful. He showed up in his wheelchair with the cutest little bald head I'd ever seen. He was shy until I started talking about his favorite football team, and then his eyes lit up like the brightest star. I followed his journey over the next several months. I wrote a book titled "Angels Yell Roll Tide" as a gift to the family. The greatest unconditional love I've seen in my life was the love the parents of these kids who were terminally ill had for their children. They never complained about the hundreds of hospital visits, the mounting bills, the time it took to care for them, or the pain their children faced. They just loved God, put faith in His love, and took one day at a time... as precious time was all they had left with their children.

Cherish your time with your loved ones. Help others. Build your personal brand for the right reasons.

If you take one thing away from this book, please take away that you are worthy of having your own personal brand. Everyone has one. What each of us decides to do with our talents is up to us. Only you can decide how to make a positive impact on the lives of others to make this world a better place.

Love,

QB Darla

Bonus: QB Darla has included daily motivations that she has written over the years for you. It's a gift from her to you. Read one a day to lift your spirits!

Follow QB Darla for fun videos, life advice, and authentic stories.

QB Darla's Daily Motivation

I've written these messages and created videos on my social media over the last 15 years to inspire others to believe in themselves, to find joy, and to maximize their days on earth. I've compiled them here for you to get a daily dose of QB Darla.

One a day will keep the therapist away. (Maybe not, but I tried to at least put a smile on your face.)

TIME IS A GIFT

Spend it wisely.

Don't waste it worrying about things you can't control.

Spend it gracefully.

Pour into those who need someone to love them.

Spend it carefully.

If something doesn't bring you joy, do less of it.

Spend it honestly.

Be true to yourself and others.

Spend it adventurously.

Explore places and things that enlighten you.

Spend it faithfully.

Hold strong to your beliefs, but love others who think differently.

Spend it curiously.

Allow your imagination to run wild and learn new things.

Spend it lovingly.

Accept people who are different.

Spend it happily.

Find what makes you smile. Do more of it.

Time is a gift. Cherish it.

REJECTION IS OK

Rejection is hard. Most of us face it. I've seen rejection in many forms...relationships, promotions, jobs, and sports.

The best way to overcome rejection is to remember these three things.

1-Rejection makes you more sympathetic and humble. If you can learn from the reason you were rejected, you can become a more compassionate person. Humility with strength is a great combination.

2- Rejection isn't always personal. Take it to heart and digest it. Then, hold your head high and conquer new things.

3- Rejection makes you smarter. If you research why you were rejected, you can become wiser going into your next challenge in life.

YOU'VE GOT THIS!

A simple "I'm sorry" goes a long way to finding peace.

It's two words that are strong enough to heal animosity between friends.

It's humbling yourself enough to admit you did something wrong or something you wish you had done differently.

It's showing others that you are imperfect, and that's OK.

It's a way to validate someone else's feelings. You don't have to be right all the time.

It's having the courage to be humble and reflective.

It's a strong personality trait to show humility because if you're able to identify both your strengths and weaknesses, you have the power to be better. Taking ownership is strong.

It's a way to de-escalate tension so positive results and communication can happen.

It's a way to mend hurt, settle disagreements, and break down barriers.

It's a peaceful feeling. Sincerity heals wounds. Find joy.

Life is short. Let's spend it peacefully.

It's OK not to be OK.

ARE YOU STRUGGLING WITH ANYTHING TODAY?

Here are a few things to do to get out of the funk!

1- Talk to someone. Share your pains with someone you can trust. Try not to air your frustrations out on other people or on social media. Instead, find ways to help your cause in a constructive way.

2- Change up your routine. Include things you enjoy in your day, like indulging in hobbies, calling those you love and who love you back, and listening to uplifting songs and podcasts. Read encouraging posts. Watch a funny movie.

3- Get outside. Walk, exercise, and chase the sun. On a cloudy day, create your own sunshine or watch content that makes you smile.

4-Pray, meditate, or find a quiet space to journal or reflect. Turn your worries over, but work hard to overcome challenges.

5-Give back. Realize that there are kids getting chemo today, men/women who have been given a limited number of days to live, people who cannot afford to put food on their tables, parents dealing with drugs, those going through abuse, and many other problems.

6- Problems are typically temporary. Time heals. Fight hard to find some kind of happiness every single day. Every person is different, so be yourself and be proud of the things you do. Then, be determined to do a little more to improve your life and others' lives every day.

7- Take deep breaths. Hit the reset button. Celebrate the little things. It's OK to not be OK, but do something to get out of the funk.

PAIN TO POWER

How do we allow our pain to become our power?

Pain hurts. Whether it's physical or emotional, it hurts the same.

Tears are real. Tears can feel surreal. Tears can help heal.

Loneliness is hard. Relationships can cause your heart to be guarded.

Loss can be tough. Something missing is often rough. The absence screams at us.

Take a pause and embrace that it's OK to be sad, lonely, and lost.

It's OK to have moments of doubt, worry, and anger.

Trust in yourself and commit to allowing your pain to become your power. The people you've lost would want you to overcome and embrace your power and gifts.

· Make one healthier choice in your daily routine to connect to nature.

· Allow others to pour into your life. Commit to watching content that makes you feel alive. Thrive.

- Allow yourself some grace, time to reflect and heal, and work towards finding joy in your way on your own timeframe.
- As you overcome and learn more about yourself, the pain will transition into your own power.
- Recognize your pain, but allow progress without feeling guilty.

Over time, that pain will lead to power.

Confidence will come. Passion will prevail. Your mission will be revealed.

Be yourself and own who you are! You are more than enough.

You are powerful!

Do more.

Today, you are going to manifest a great day. You're going to do more, love more, give more, sell more, create more, innovate more, lift more, eat healthier foods, drink healthy drinks, exercise more, learn more, give more thanks, more smiles, and more compliments.

Let's go. You can do this. Do more for you, your loved ones, your creator, co-workers, owner, friends, and yourself!

BUILD YOUR FORCE FIELD

Why is it important to build a strong force field around you?

1- Protection-it's a shield of armor as you go into the battle of life's ongoing challenges

2- Encouragement- it's a sphere of those who want you to win

3- Affirmation- it's a catalyst for great innovation and creativity

4- Influence- its power to help others

5- Appreciation- it's two-way thankfulness for each other

How do you select people and things to be a part of that bubble?

1- Faith- God is my rock for prayer, wisdom, strength, and grace

2- Family, friends & community—family first, followed by those who have similar values, those who are imperfect yet helpful, smart yet humble, kind, and encouraging. Those who enjoy nature, fitness, or hobbies you enjoy.

3- Content: small doses of negative news, large doses of positive news. Lots of humor, hobbies, travel, and content to build your dreams.

4- Tools: books, podcasts, those who use knowledge to strengthen others

5- Work- find mentors who help you get over your fears, who truly believe in you

6-No drama- walk away from the "tea."

Building your force field and pouring into those who pour into you is important. Be that friend who builds people up instead of tearing them down. Be the co-worker who leads others to greatness. Be that community person who gets involved with helping others. Be the one who is OK with being different by making choices that may not be the most popular. Be a world-changer.

Don't stay in your little bubble because it's healthy to help others and see other people's problems. It's good to be compassionate to those around you. It's healthy to see new things.

Your force field will give you the strength and confidence to do great things beyond what you believe you can do yourself.

Your field may change over time. There will be those that come and go, and that's OK. You'll learn life lessons from the good and the bad. Use those lessons to improve yourself over time.

Wrap your arms around people who don't have a force field. Show them love and encouragement.

PASSION IGNITES AMBITION

Ambition stimulates action. Action generates results.

Example: In 2012, I started a publishing business to help kids in hospitals who were going through cancer or other illnesses. I donated over 50k books to kids across the country. That passion for those kids, along with my three sons, has led me to public speaking, meaningful work that I dedicate myself to, and inventions I help bring to life.

Every day, I get up and think about what fuels my fire, then I take action and expect results.

Passion doesn't allow you to quit. Passion propels you forward.

WORK-LIFE BALANCE

It's important to be consistently happy. Finding true joy is going to look different for everyone. For me, it's spending quality time with my three boys, maintaining a job, and always striving for more in business, faith in God, motivating others to believe in themselves, and giving back. To maintain a healthy work-life balance, I do the following things:

-Prioritize my family

-Organize my work ahead of time

-Keep my eye on the prize

-Take swift action to get things done

-Have fun every day

-Compliment others and help them win

-Surround myself with positive people

-Exercise and take care of my body and mind

-Compete and stay ahead of my competition

-Add value in every situation

-Never settle

-Create ongoing, ever-changing goals

-Constantly learn and listen

-Look for adventures (travel, see cool places, do neat things)

BUILD BRIDGES, NOT WALLS

A bridge is a structure built to span physical obstacles such as bodies of water, valleys, or roads, providing passage over the obstacle.

Bridges are designed to support various loads, including pedestrians, vehicles, and trains.

They can be made from different materials, such as wood, stone, steel, and concrete. Like humans, we are built with different personalities, looks, habits, and opinions.

Bridges are supported by beams and arches, and we need people around us to support us through life's challenges.

"Hey, sweet lady! Thought you would be happy to know Braxton and Bentlee were both accepted into Alabama's honors college! They are so excited. Both got scholarships as well! Thank you for loving my babies like you did when they were growing up! We will never forget you!"

This message from a cancer survivor's mom meant the world to me.

Let's all build bridges, not walls.

ONE GREAT THING

Focus on one great thing you accomplished today. On a given day, you may do many things wrong and a few things right. Don't beat yourself up. Learn from the mistakes and become better. Concentrate on the one great thing that happened to you today, and use that positive energy to do more good in the coming days.

Golfers often make a ton of mistakes, but they remember the best shot they had that day. That's what they talk about, and it fuels them to play again.

Musicians hit lots of wrong notes, but when they produce that number one single, it fuels them to keep writing and making music.

Fishermen sit around all day trying to catch the big one. They finally get one on the hook to realize it's too small to keep... or it's a shoe someone lost in the water. They finally catch one fish, and that's what they talk about, and it grows bigger each time they tell the story. But... they look forward to getting back out there!

Business leaders make wrong decisions on a daily basis. Every now and then, they hit a winner that saves their company money or increases profit. Every once in a while, they see someone excel and light up because of what they have taught them. They allow the wins to fuel their fire for greatness, and they are eager to lead again tomorrow.

Today, I encourage you to concentrate on the wins of your day. Hold your head high and thrive tomorrow because of the small successes today.

Allow 1 great thing each day to light your fire going into tomorrow.

You don't have to be better than everyone else. You just need to strive to better yourself every single day.

Get ready to tackle another day and bring positive energy vibes to everyone in your path.

TURBULENCE

Today, as I was flying back home, we experienced a little turbulence in the air. It made me think about the fact that a lot of people haven't had it easy. Some people may experience an easy life with very few bumps. However, most of us face trials that feel overwhelming at times. We may feel like we can't catch a break. We work long hours, and we put in the effort and time with no reward. We may watch others succeed, and we're in the same place as we were ten years ago.

I'd like to offer this positive energy to you. Stay the course. If you take a look around, you might realize that your hard work is paying off if you have a roof over your head and food on your table. You are fortunate if you are healthy. If you choose negative energy, you'll attract negative people. If you choose positive energy, you'll attract positive people.

Sometimes, we can't control the events in our lives. We can choose how we perceive and react to them. We can figure out healthy ways to cope with hardships or rocky roads.

Choose to smile. Choose to offer compliments instead of complaints. Choose to believe in yourself. Choose to be a light in the dark. Choose to keep working hard to chase your dreams. Choose to surround yourself with positive energy and uplifting people. Choose positive thoughts. Choose to dream instead of giving up. Choose now, and don't wait for another day. Today is that day. Choose YOU. Then, choosing those you love becomes easier.

ABCs FOR A POSITIVE MINDSET

A: Attitude & effort determine outcomes.

B: Be bold and do not fear failure.

C: Challenge yourself by learning new things daily.

D: Determination brings results.

E: Effort trumps laziness.

F: Follow through gets deals done.

G: Growth comes when you expand your thinking beyond what you think you are capable of.

H: High-five others and pay compliments.

I: Ignite the fire and find your passion.

J: Jump at opportunities even if you are afraid.

K: Kick some booty daily. Earn the gifts you receive.

L: Legacy is more than money and the gifts you leave. It's the lessons and values you provide right now. Pour into others and build yours to last.

M: Mistakes are often mistaken for failure. Allow them to fuel you.

N: Need balance of work, fun, giving, love, and growth.

O: Open doors to see which one is the right one for you. Many will close. Push harder. Be determined.

P: Persistence usually pays off.

Q: Quit pouring negative content into your daily routine. Surround yourself with positive content that motivates you.

R: Relax and celebrate the goodness around you. Enjoy the ride!

S: Stay consistently happy by having hobbies you enjoy, people you love around you, and a good balance of work/life.

T: Take the initiative and put in the work on yourself and your goals.

U: Ultimately, you choose how you spend your time. Time is a gift.

V: Vocalize your outcomes. Envision the end results.

W: Winners compete. Win humbly, yet be proud. Lose with grace and learn how to be better.

X: Xtra. Be extraordinary.

Y: You are worthy. You are unique. You are capable.

&

Z: Zoom into the next phase of your life with passion and excitement.

WE ONLY GET ONE LIFE

Now, I'm not suggesting that you get complacent with your work habits. Sometimes, our worries and mistakes drive us to greatness if we learn to get past the hard part. I'm suggesting that you stay uber-focused on the things that produce the most results. Surround yourself with people who build you up. Tune in to content that gives you a feeling of learning or accomplishing good things. Dream those dreams. Take action on your ideas. We have one life. Don't turn to vices when the going gets tough. Instead, do things that strengthen your mind, body, and soul. Fuel your passion. We get one chance to make a difference in this world. Make it count.

RISE TO THE CHALLENGE

Are you going to allow small things in your life to defeat you? No!

Will you let negative people influence your thoughts? No!

Can you continue allowing yourself to doubt your abilities, looks, and mindset? No!

Should you blame others for things that don't go your way all the time? No!

Are you ready to RISE to the CHALLENGE?

If you are, please commit to these things:

1- Find one way to make someone smile each day

2- Change your routine and include physical activity, fitness, dance, walking, or whatever gets your blood flowing

3- Create a music playlist – anything upbeat and fun that you can listen to when you start to feel blue.

4- Surround yourself with positive people and lessen the amount of media and negative things in your life.

You control the things and people you spend time with, your activities and choices, and your mindset.

You have the power to be extraordinary. The power to make changes for the better.

...to surround yourself with positivity.

...work hard to make a living.

...do things outside of your comfort zone.

...forgive others and start a new day.

...make healthy choices.

...remove yourself from uncomfortable situations.

...find peace in your life.

...be who you are meant to be.

...to be extraordinary.

Live strong

Love hard.

Forgive often.

Win humbly.

Lose gracefully.

Learn daily.

Compliment consistently.

Adapt accordingly.

Persevere fiercely.

Laugh uncontrollably.

Believe wholeheartedly.

Give graciously.

Visualize Good Outcomes

When you wake up, try visualizing some positive outcomes for your life.

(What do you want to achieve for your loved ones, yourself, your work, and your future? What do you want people to say about you when you aren't around?)

-family

-work

-personal

-legacy

Then write down a few mulligans you need to forgive yourself or others for before you move on.

(Who do you need to forgive? What things do you need to forgive yourself for?)

-forgive

-let go

-redo

Now, define success.

(What is success, as most others see it? What does success mean to you?)

-world's definition

-YOUR definition

Finally, think about some kind of selfless giving in your plans.

(How can I give back to others in a selfless way with no expectation of getting anything back? What is my passion?)

-charity

-giving time, $, energy

If you visualize it, you can do it. If you do it, you can achieve it. If you achieve it, you will spread the joy to others. If you improve the lives of others, you will build a strong legacy to outlast you. Show grace to yourself and to others. Start now. It's never too late.

Treat every day like a special occasion!

BUILDING RELATIONSHIPS

Be Yourself

-Each of you has your own unique qualities. Every single person is created for a purpose. You may still be exploring life and looking for answers, but they will come. Your purpose doesn't have to be extravagant. It doesn't have to shout from the depths of social media. It just needs to be whatever you think is important in life. That thing that makes your heart beat faster. The reason you rise and shine. The "get up and go" to your day. The peanut butter to your jelly.

Don't rely on other people to make you great because they don't have the same DNA or fingerprint as you. There is a 1 in 64B chance you have the same fingerprint as someone else.

And don't look to other people to make you feel like you are great. There's only one YOU. Imperfections throughout our lives are part of who we are. We utilize those to learn and grow stronger.

Trust me, you are GREAT.

Be genuine.

-People like to be around people who exude strength, positivity, and humility.

Know your strengths and acknowledge your weaknesses.

-List your strengths

(Talk about them)

-List your weaknesses

(Talk about them)

Stay consistently happy.

-Not too high, not too low

-Hard times are temporary

Take care of yourself so you can give back to others.

-Exercise

-Get outside

-Hobbies (sports, reading, fishing, gardening, hunting, skydiving, hiking...)

-Nutrition

-Sleep

-Giving back

-Proactive check-ups

-Breathe

-Humor is necessary

-Surround yourself with positive people, less negative input (you are what you eat)

-If you get into a rut, change your routine

-Take a break

-Small support groups

-Accept help

If it doesn't give you joy, do less of it.

Treat people with respect. Everyone has something to offer.

Focus on the good. Acknowledge hard times but realize it's temporary, and don't get sucked into negative feelings day after day. Dig out of it.

Control your thoughts. Mind over matter.

Give yourself credit where credit is due. When you accomplish something, it's ok to feel proud. Life is hard sometimes. Celebrate the small wins along the way.

Commit to compliment someone every day. Your co-workers, family, spouse, kids, strangers....

BE PRESENT

Have you ever been talking to someone, and they are constantly getting distracted by everything around them?

Guilty! My brain works nonstop, coming up with ideas, solutions to problems, ways to do things better, innovations, impact I want to make, meeting everyone around me, and a million other things.

Suggestions (which I'm learning as well):

1-When going out to dinner, leave your phone in the car. Gulp! Really? Oh shoot... that's going to be tough. I'm truly addicted to it. But... I'm going to try it. Will you?

2- Try to remember the color of the person's eyes an hour after you leave them.

3- Try to write down three "takeaways" that are about the person who is with you. Things like...what makes them happy, what motivates them, who are their mentors, what hobbies do they enjoy...you get the picture.

4- Ask questions about them because you care and want to know their heart.

5- Talk about their future goals. What do they want to accomplish? Where do they see themselves in a few years?

6- Laugh with them. Cry with them. Hug them. Cheer them up.

7- Do more listening. Don't listen to react. Listen to care deeply.

Let's help each other learn, grow, love, and be present in the moment.

How can I be better today?

Time is precious. Sometimes, we hear of people leaving this early, too soon. Our eyes are opened to the reality that death is real. And, it is real hard on our hearts to accept the person has passed because they are loved.

LET'S SELF-REFLECT TODAY

What am I going to do today to make sure my family knows they are loved?

Is there an act of kindness that will make a stranger smile today?

Do I need to forgive someone?

Can I create something to make an impact on the world?

Will I make phone calls instead of texts to say I love you?

Is someone else's time more important than mine?

Should I read something that will help my positivity or watch something negative?

If my team loses, will I be humble and realize that it's just a game?

Will I add something healthy instead of unhealthy to my daily routine?

Let's live life with the intention of loving others NOW, not later. Let's put our own wants aside for a minute and focus on what someone else needs. If mistakes have been made, forgive yourself and move on to do something great. Let's not be caught with any regrets. Let's start loving and forgiving ourselves so we can have the capacity to love and forgive others.

HOW CAN I BE BETTER TODAY?

Time is precious. ❤❤❤ Hugs to all of my friends who have experienced loss. May your hearts grow stronger each day, and the memories make you thankful.

Do you have any tips that work for you?

I know I can

If I know I can, I will.

If I know I will, I won't doubt myself.

If I avoid distractions, I will prosper.

If I prosper, those I love will benefit.

If I think positive, I can do anything.

If I can do anything, then nothing is too difficult to overcome.

If I believe in myself, I can handle any obstacle.

If I handle any obstacle, the hard things get easier.

If I get in the zone, I will seize the day.

If I seize the day, my productivity will go through the roof.

If I achieve hard things, I will feel proud.

If I feel proud, I'm able to help others feel proud.

If I smile, I will uplift others.

If I uplift others, my day will be brighter.

If I know I can, I will!

I know I can!

YOUR VIBE

Today, focus on your vibe. Your vibe is the energy you reflect on yourself and others around you.

If it's dull, sharpen it.

If it's mad, do things that make you happy.

If it's jealous, swallow your pride and learn from others.

If it's boring, liven it up.

If it's judging others, allow humility to open your eyes.

Exude to others the energy you'd like to be around. Open your heart to be kind to others. Make your vibe something you can be proud of.

COUNT WHAT COUNTS

Count your joys instead of your pains.

Count your gain instead of your pain.

Count your blessings instead of your stresses.

Count your friends instead of your foes.

Count your happiness instead of your woes.

Count your courage instead of your fears.

Count your smiles instead of your tears.

LOOK FOR THE GOOD

I don't care what you look like...

It doesn't matter what you wear.

The color of your hair.

I don't care what is in your past...

It doesn't matter what mistakes you've made.

Judgment won't be cast.

I don't care about your flaws.

We've all got our own.

Positive vibes are what draw.

I'll look for the good in you.

I'll cheer for you to win.

I'll challenge you to be your best.

Each and every day.

We are blessed.

When you run into me...

I promise you this.

The hug is real, and the words are true.

Every conversation, interaction, or message I've had with you.

I read them, cherish them, and am so thankful for your friendship.

I challenge you today to look for the good in people.

We are all different for a reason.

SECOND GUESSING

Do you second-guess your every move? Let me help you think through this...

1- Fear creates disbelief in ourselves. Be fearless sometimes, and just go for it.

2- If you are doing something good that you believe in, have faith that it will work out, and then work hard to make it happen.

3- At times, you have got to just go with your gut. Your first instinct is often a solid choice.

4- Research and prepare. If you do that, then you are more apt to trust yourself.

5- Do the darn thing. I know some things can be scary and out of your comfort zone, but be willing to go that extra mile if you have an idea that you are contemplating, a trip you want to take, a person you want to meet, a challenge you want to face, a task you want to complete, a job you want to apply for, a business you want to start, etc.

Life is too short to continually second-guess yourself because you don't believe in your gifts. Yes, YOU have gifts!

TATTERED & TORN, BUT INVINCIBLE

You may have been heartbroken, but your heart can heal over time.

You may be uncertain, but you can gain confidence.

You may be struggling with work, but you can overcome obstacles.

You may be afraid, but you can do hard things.

You have experienced loss, but you are loved.

You may have messed up, but you can learn and grow from it.

You may feel bummed, but tomorrow is a new day.

You may feel inadequate, but you are just enough.

You may feel tattered and torn, but YOU are invincible.

RESPECT

A feeling of admiring someone or something that is good, valuable, important, etc.

Please show respect for those around you. More than likely, they have done something to earn the respect you are about to give them. If not, showing respect will hopefully encourage them to do something in their life to earn it in their future.

R-E-S-P-E-C-T keeps everyone happy.

It's healthy to be happy when others win. I want everyone around me to win!

There's no room for jealousy and envy. There's plenty of room for everyone to win at something.

If you're early, you're on time. If you're on time, you're late. Everyone else's time is just as important as yours.

Time is a gift we are given. We shouldn't assume we'll get more, so let's max out what we have.

-Earn what you get.

-Be thankful for those who help you.

-Be grateful for people who treat you right.

-Forgive those who have done you wrong.

-Try to resist the temptation to talk negatively about others.

The bottom line is to respect and treat people as you want to be treated.

BE EXTRA

In everything that you do, give a little bit of extra effort.

Do what you think you can do. Then, push yourself to do EXTRA.

EXTRA.

Every single day.

EXTRA.

All the time.

EXTRA.

In every circumstance.

ANTICIPATE

Solutions don't come from people who sit around and do nothing. Things happen when you plan ahead. Actions get results.

Quick Tips:

-Think well beyond the outcome

-Always think about adding value

-Be a step ahead of your competition

-Ask "what if"

-Solve problems

-Be dependable so people can trust you and count on your choices

-Choose a lifestyle that makes you more productive

-Research

-Don't assume

-Ask the questions

-Commit to learn from mistakes and figure out ways to become better in all aspects of your life

-Be consistent with your actions

-Take responsibility for your mistakes and ask for feedback

-Don't take complaints personally

-Strive for your own version of greatness

Do you want to get results? Do you want to be a step ahead or lag behind?

If you anticipate and think ahead, this positive mentality will serve you well. This philosophy applies to business, life, parenting, and relationships.

Think ahead. Use your noggin'!

YOU ARE JUST ENOUGH

You are flawed

Imperfect

You are scarred

Worn

You have experienced hurt

Torn

You are capable

Able

You are a fighter

Fierce

You are ready to overcome

Powerful

You will not let fear defeat you

Strong

You are worth it

Worthy

You are just enough

Satisfied

ONE DAY

We are given one day at a time

...to shine ...to define ...to climb

Shine your light on high beam

Define yourself and your desires, and climb that hurdle

What will you do with your day?

...say ...pray ...don't be afraid.

Say the things you mean, pray with conviction, and don't be afraid to take chances. 24 hours is not a lot of time, but it becomes a lifetime if it's all you have left. It becomes that day you wish you had made more of it if it slips away. Make every second count.

We are given one day at a time

...to reach ...to help ...to love

Reach for the highest goal

Help others reach their potential

Love fiercely

What will you do with your day?

...do ...move ...don't lose hope

Take action and be a doer

Keep moving

Never ever lose hope

Someday, we will all pass

Today, let's make love last

Make your one day full of impact

You'll never get that one day back

Dance!

ONE LIFE

How many times have you wanted to do something but didn't because of the fear of failure? Fear of what others would think? Fear of the unknown? Fear of rejection?

You have ONE life. You don't know how much time you have left.

There are some nuggets to consider:

-If you are reading this, you are breathing.

-If you are breathing, you are blessed.

-If you are blessed, you are capable of doing things.

-If you do things, you are living.

-If you are living, you can give back.

-If you give back, you are making the world a better place.

-If the world is better because of you, you will impact the next generation.

-If you impact lives, your legacy will not be forgotten.

Live life every single day like you mean it. Experience new things. Do the things you yearn for. Find joy in the little things. Leave the drama behind. Love those around you. Tell people what you want them to know. Embrace change.

Dance!

Don't ever give up!

A FOREVER FAN

One of my friends told me about a concert by 8 Seconds Saloon, and I had never heard of the artist. I listened to a few songs in my car to prepare for the show and immediately loved his voice and lyrics. Little did I know, I was in for a big surprise. It became my all-time favorite concert for these reasons:

1- Drake White is an incredible singer, musician, and performer.

2- He captures your heart by telling his story about how he had to learn how to walk again and was determined to get back on stage to share his music.

3- He inspires his audience with messages of faith and resilience. He encourages people to look at his miracle and never give up. He lives with his wife, Alex, and wrote "Makin Me Look Good Again" after his dad said that to him about her.

4- His fans adore him. I now see why. I'm forever a fan. They latch on to his energy. His energy is contagious.

5- I was in the front row, and he took my phone and filmed the crowd. He shook hands afterward and thanked his

audience. He was genuine, down-to-earth, and cared about people.

Drake's story: In August 2019, Drake collapsed on stage during a performance in Virginia. He was hospitalized and found out he had an abnormal vascular formation in the brain, which constricts blood flow, called an arteriovenous malformation (AVM). He has opened for Luke Bryan, Little Big Town, and Zac Brown Band.

I was inspired by him to inspire you today with these words.

Life can be hard. Life can throw us curveballs in our health, wealth, and relationships. The most important thing we can do is keep pushing and never give up. Live life each day as if it were going to be our last. Pray and thank God for our blessings. Love those around us, no matter how different they are.

Much love to Drake White and his family. I'm forever a fan and will be attending more of his shows. I may even road trip to his barn music venue (Whitewood Hollow) in Tennessee since I'm a "Barn Gangster" now.

APPLAUD OTHERS

Can you be happy for someone who is more successful than you?

Can you be proud of someone who has a better job than you?

Can you be excited for someone who is prettier than you?

Can you compliment someone who has a great outfit on?

Can you high give someone who just accomplished something they dreamed about?

Can you shake someone's hand who has just completed a big business deal?

Can you look at someone's relationship with adornment instead of jealousy?

It's important to be comfortable with who you are so you can be genuinely happy for others.

Being content with who you are doesn't mean you shouldn't strive for more in your life. You should always try to be your best, accomplish your dreams, and make the world better.

As you are doing that, be confident and don't be jealous or afraid to give accolades to others for their accomplishments. Be proud of their wins.

Competition is healthy, but trust in your abilities and allow yourself to grow through others' strengths.

Every person has a gift. Find yours and be happy for those around you who are living out their journey.

Applaud others.

Ask

Ask for the sale.

You might get it.

Ask for the date.

You might get it.

Ask for the promotion.

You might get it.

Ask for the answers.

You might get them.

Ask for help.

You might get it.

If you don't ask, I guarantee you will not get what you want.

Instead of wishing for it, work hard for it. Ask for it. You deserve it.

BELIEVE IN ME CHECKLIST

I want each of you to believe in yourself. Be satisfied with who you are.

....I won't settle for mediocre

....I value my worth

....I learn from my mistakes

....I laugh at myself

....I find strength in my weaknesses

....I give back with no expectations

....I want others to win

....I do things for myself

....I take breaks

....I work hard

....I create a healthy balance

....I believe I can do hard things

....I continually improve

....I'm OK with my flaws

....I stay consistently happy

....I can forgive

....I am me, 100% me

SAME YET DIFFERENT

Today and every day, you are worthy of love, laughter, and living your best life.

Same yet different

It's fall, ya'll.

I may like noodles in my chili.

You may not.

I may like pumpkin spice and everything nice. You may not.

The thing is... everyone has different tastes in what they like and dislike.

Everyone has their own journey comprised of ups, downs, and all-around.

Each one of us grew up in different areas with a variety of events that impacted our lives along our journey.

Some have gone through things that others can't even imagine how they would get through them if they happened to them. The unimaginable exists.

A mom lost her teenage daughter in an automobile accident.

A man watched his best friend get killed in a war.

A young child died of cancer in his mom and dad's arms.

An Uber driver gave a homeless man his shoes off his feet which belonged to his deceased son, who passed away at an early age. He wore them to cherish the memories and gave them away when someone else needed them more.

A dad lost his job and struggled to pay his bills until someone gave him a chance.

The pain in the lives of those around us may seem unbearable, but they find the strength to forge ahead.

When you walk by someone, show them respect. You do not know what they are going through.

Acknowledge their existence and honor their story, even if you don't know what their pages consist of.

How do you know someone's story? You don't unless you ask. You don't unless you care to ask. If you don't know their story and don't ask, assume that they are worthy of a smile and that they may need more than you realize.

A simple smile or kind gesture can be the highlight of someone's day.

Give the hopeless hope. We may not all be the same, but we're not that different. Most want to be accepted, loved, and respected, no matter what the stories are.

AMAZING GRACE

Middle of nowhere town, as small as it may seem.

Big city lights, as big as they may be.

Somewhere in the middle, some reside.

Each one is unique, far and wide.

Wherever you are, know that amazing grace abounds. Love surrounds, no matter what town.

Entrepreneur, parent, and employee grinding. Working hard.

Owner, investor, celebrity, influencer. Leading the way.

God offers grace to us every day. Why shouldn't we allow ourselves and others grace?

Embrace forgiveness for things in the past. It's time to move forward.

Perfection shouldn't stand in our way from using our imperfections to mold us so that we shine bright for others.

Grace is amazing, so let's accept our flaws, learn from them, and offer grace to others. If we aren't perfect, we shouldn't expect others to be.

Live to give and forgive. After all, isn't grace amazing?

YOU ARE WORTH IT

You are worthy. You have passed your real estate exam. You continue to go through training courses, read books, listen to podcasts, set up your marketing strategies, attend events, study contracts, and craft your skills. You work long hours offering the best service for your clients. You add value by working with the best partners you can find and going that extra mile. You have chosen a great brokerage that supports you. You are ready to crush it!

1- Prepare your mind to maximize eight hours each day.

2- Wake up; adjust your routine to include something that fires you up.

3- Get into the zone... a mentally tough mind zone. A "nothing is going to stop you" mode.

4- Tackle the day like the boss that you were meant to be.

5- Prioritize the most profitable, productive, and important things first. Get them done. Action gets results.

6- Know your value and negotiate firm because you know you are worth it.

Go crush it! You are worthy.

HEARTS HEAL

If you are going through a breakup, stay strong. It won't be long until your heart heals.

Sometimes, God knows the right person for you when even you think you have it all figured out. Let him lead the way.

During the healing process, focus on yourself. Think about your strengths and weaknesses. We all have both.

Time heals your wounds, so recognize that you won't feel like your heart is ripped out of your chest forever.

Someone out there always has it worse. Use this lesson to make you more resilient.

There's always a plan. A plan that you need to watch unfold as you go through even the toughest times.

Patience is often overlooked. When you get lonely, find more hobbies.

Strengthen your heart by helping other people's hearts.

A heart can be filled with laughter and love from friends and family, so allow them to fill your cup up. Surround yourself with people who lift you up.

Work hard to be independent, so you don't need a relationship to be happy. If you can stand on your own, you will be more confident.

Don't give up on love; just figure out what you want and what you are willing to give, and don't settle for anything less.

Loss is hard, but the future can be bright with what is to come.

Hearts heal. You can do it.

7.9 BILLION REASONS WHY TO TRY

What if we all just try to live each day just a little bit better than we did the day before? If all 7.9 billion of us are committed to some type of self-improvement each day, imagine how much healthier the world would be.

-Take one step forward at a time.

-Don't try to change too many things at once.

-Strive for your personal best each day.

-Pick something different to work on each time you accomplish a personal goal.

-Celebrate your achievements.

-Hold yourself accountable.

-Have fun making your life better and ultimately, everyone else's around you.

-Be mentally tough to defeat the hard things.

Every day, strive to do your part to make the world a better place.

YOU ARE WORTH IT

You are worthy. You have overcome many obstacles. You have persevered through tough times. You have weathered storms. You have been knocked down and got back up. You have grown, studied, done good things, and learned valuable lessons. Now, it's time to believe in your value.

1- Prepare your mind to maximize eight hours each day.

2- Wake up. Adjust your routine to include something that fires you up.

3- Get into the zone... a mentally tough mind zone. A "nothing is going to stop you" mode.

4- Tackle the day like the boss that you were meant to be.

5- Prioritize the most profitable, productive, and important things first. Get them done. Action gets results.

6- Know your value and negotiate everything in life firm because you know you are worth it.

Go crush it! You are worthy.

Roll on!

The world is made up of all kinds of people with different backgrounds. Everyone has a different style. We are all unique. We all go through various transitions as we grow older.

If you are living your life to the fullest every single moment, you should be satisfied. Look in the mirror and be content with who you were meant to be.

Scars, flaws, imperfections, hardships, and pain can impact our journey. The important thing is to not allow those hard things to deter us from maximizing our ability to impact the world.

We have been chosen to do great things. Only we can live those gifts out by working hard, believing in ourselves, and taking action.

SELF-WORTH IS WORTH FIGHTING FOR

I choose to use my gifts to impact other people's lives. I choose to work hard. I choose to live every second to the fullest because I have seen young lives taken too soon. I choose to love people... lots of people. Yes, I'm learning to dance on roller skates. Why not? Life is worth living large.

Let's choose to be happy for ourselves and for those around us. When we find inner happiness that is not dependent on other people or things, we can then create an atmosphere where we give more than we take. We can treat others the way we want to be treated. We can find true happiness that is fulfilling for the long term.

Roll on!

STORMS SHALL PASS

Storms blow into our lives unexpectedly. Winds. Damage.

Lightning strikes, warning us of what's ahead. Bolts. Streaks.

Thunder rolls like the sound of a freight train. Crash. Boom.

Rain causes flooding. Tears. Pain.

We are made to be resilient and get through the rough weather. Fight. Push.

No one said life would be easy. Peaks. Valleys.

The world is better when we are supportive of each other. United. Together.

Show compassion for those who are weathering storms in their lives. Support. Kindness.

If we stand together, there's nothing we can get past. Resilience. Forward.

Storms shall pass, and we should remember to respect others going through difficult times. Help. Commit.

We are lucky to be alive. Live. Love.

Compliment someone today. Challenge. Accepted.

THE OTHER SIDE OF FEAR

What's on the other side of fear?

Success.

Health.

Life.

Love.

Freedom.

Impact.

When you were a kid, did you live in fear? No. Did you let fear hold you back? No. Why would you allow fear to hold you back now? Fear less. Live more.

LEARN CONSTANTLY

Sharpen your skills at something every single day. One business skill that I have tried to sharpen is listening to people's needs. When you care about the customer's needs first and foremost, the selling becomes fun because you are providing necessary solutions to help them accomplish their goals.

Pick something you want to learn in your personal life and work on that.

Cheers to learning new things for personal and business growth every single day!

YOU ARE STRONG

You are strong. You carry heavy loads.

Your heart beats fast for those you love. You hurt when others hurt.

You have experienced loss. Your soul is missing a piece of what previously existed.

Your happiness has been shaken.

The devastation left doubt in your mind.

But through it all, you can find the strength to move forward. Strength to carry others with you. Strength to improve what has been lost or broken.

People like you, who have experienced hard things and learned how to grow from them, need to help others thrive. The world needs you.

When you help others, you heal. Your hurt becomes tolerable. Your heart is filled with joy. Your pain may not go away, but you can overcome what you think is impossible.

You've got this! You can carry a heavy load as long as you surround yourself with the right people who will cheer you on. Take one day at a time. Use your story to make an impact.

MISSED OPPORTUNITIES

I'm a big believer that God puts people in our lives for special purposes. Each time I meet a stranger, I wonder if I'm supposed to meet them for a specific reason. Am I supposed to help them? Is there a reason I have crossed paths with them? My curious mind has led me to meet some unbelievable people who have become very meaningful to me. I've been known to plop myself right in between strangers and become lifelong friends.

Let's stop and think about each person we meet this week and how we might be able to impact their life in a positive way. Most of the time, we'll never know the other person's story because we're too busy to ask.

Intuition

Meets

Passion

Admiration

Compassion

Timing

Scenario: A young teenage driver hits your car on the way to work.

Response A: Get mad and yell at her.

Response B: Cuss at her, calm down, then kick dirt on her car.

Response C: Think before you act... "She made a mistake, and I'm sure she feels bad enough, so I'm not going to make her feel worse. Maybe I was supposed to meet her to show her kindness and forgiveness. I'm thankful everyone is safe." Let the authorities and insurance companies do their jobs.

Which one do you think would have a bigger impact? Why? (What you didn't know was that this girl's mom just passed away two days earlier, and she was crying on her way to her job. She found out her dog had cancer, and she just had her hours cut back at work.)

How many missed opportunities have we had and haven't realized them? It's never too late to start recognizing them. IMPACT lives.

Change starts with every interaction where we encounter a stranger who is trying to do their best.

Love so hard that it hurts.

Give so much that you lose sleep.

Help so much that you have zero regrets at the end of each day.

I've been blessed to be able to help others through my books. They have opened me up to a world that I may have never known.

Now, it's a mission that I have to help heal people's hurt through the simple gift of time, a hug, a smile, a donation, a book, a connection, or words of inspiration.

Life has taught me a few things:

1- When you open yourself to those who hurt, you help them and become a stronger person.

2- Every person is unique and has their own story to tell. I want to hear it all, see it all, and help as many people as I can.

3- Kids are resilient. They are blessed with the gift to get through pain and hardships. They amaze me.

4- Adults need to learn from kids. We need to be nicer to each other and open our eyes to the real world.

5- We need to remember what is important. We need to love hard, live fiercely, and help others.

YOU ARE ENOUGH!

Energetic people

Never give up

On their dreams

Ultimately,

Good things will

Happen.

Rise Above It.

When struggles come,

You can win the fight.

Tomorrow is a new day,

Your day will shine bright.

When you feel beaten down,

You think you are going to fail.

Keep looking up.

You will prevail.

When your heart is broken,

Know that time will heal the pain.

Stay the course. Don't be afraid.

Believe in love again.

When your world turns upside down,

A little faith goes a long way.

There is hope.

No matter what others may say.

When you fall, use that as a sign.

A big, bold reminder to fight.

Embrace the climb.

Dark turns to light.

There are no guarantees.

Take whatever life throws your way.

Rise above it with a smile.

Seize your moment every single day.

You are important to someone.

Aren't we all lucky to be alive?

The influence is in your hands.

You are being watched by many eyes.

Do what's right.

Right, what's wrong.

Dance that dance.

Sing that song.

Most of all, don't live with regrets.

Show love, kindness & good deeds.

Take action to mend the hurt.

Water the earth and plant new seeds.

Take chances.

Rise above it!

Live bold and take nothing for granted.

Life is too legit to quit!

BE THE SUNSHINE

Think about your life right now. Are you giving back? Are you sharing your knowledge with others? Are you living as bold as you can live? Are you challenging yourself at home and at work? Are you being the sunshine on a rainy day for others?

Here are a few tips to be the sunshine on a cloudy day:

1- Wake up and play your favorite tunes.

2- Live to impact others' lives.

3- Turn the page of fear and start writing a new chapter on things you will overcome.

4- Realize your gifts and share them.

5- Work hard and dream larger than you can imagine.

6-Surround yourself with people who build you up, not tear you down.

7- Listen to uplifting people, limit your exposure to negativity, and shine your light bright.

8- Volunteer or help someone in need. A life where you open yourself up to see pain makes you compassionate, so you can appreciate life.

9- Love yourself and cheer on others to win. There is no room for jealousy when your heart is full.

10- Believe that you can do hard things because difficult things are possible to overcome and accomplish. Be resilient.

BUTTERFLY KISSES FROM HEAVEN

Doctor says it will be alright.

We need a miracle to shine down tonight.

Will you impact the world with the words you say?

One thousand days, one thousand ways.

Moments so precious,

Every day, we get a fresh start.

Nothing will ever

Pull us apart.

Be strong.

It won't be long.

Fight.

Until the end of time.

Butterfly Kisses from Heaven

You've shown me a new way.

Land on my face and make things clear.

Flying all around me, up, up, and away.

No one knows how life will go.

Only time will tell.

So make the most of your time here.

Smile for a while...

Sweet kisses on my cheek.

Bright colors of butterflies.

Landing on my skin.

Fly so high. So high.

Imagine with me

A California wave

An Indiana breeze

Will you please stay?

Love.

From Heaven above.

Survive.

Be alive and thrive.

Butterfly Kisses from Heaven

You've shown me a new way.

Land on my face and make things clear.

Flying all around me, up, up, and away.

Anything can happen

Just believe.

Footprints in the sand

So much to achieve

YOU ARE GREAT

Each of you has your own unique qualities. Every single person is created for a purpose. You may still be exploring life and looking for answers, but they will come. Your purpose doesn't have to be extravagant. It doesn't have to shout from the depths of social media. It just needs to be whatever you think is important in life. That thing that makes your heart beat faster. The reason you rise and shine. The "get up and go" to your day. The peanut butter to your jelly.

YOU ARE GREAT

Don't rely on other people to make you great because they don't have the same DNA or fingerprint as you. And don't look to other people to make you feel like you are great. There's only one YOU. Imperfections throughout our lives are part of who we are. We utilize those to learn and grow stronger. Failures are temporary.

Trust me, you are GREAT.

Crush It!

Here are a few tips to CRUSH it:

1- Prepare your mind to maximize eight hours each day.

2- Wake up and change your routine to include something that fires you up.

3- Get into the zone... a mentally tough mind zone. A "nothing is going to stop me" mode.

4- Tackle the day like the boss that you were meant to be.

5- Prioritize the most profitable, productive, and important things first. Get them done.

GO CRUSH IT!

Dance, Leap, Dream

Live life every day to the fullest.

Forget the past.

Forgive.

Live life to make an impact.

Others count.

Care.

Kiss and hug your family often.

Tell them.

Love.

Take risks, and don't let fear rule.

Challenge yourself.

Leap.

Dance because you feel the energy.

Have fun.

Boogie.

Dream large and be in charge.

Try it.

Drive.

Allow passion to fuel your fire.

Align your heart.

Burn.

Smile at the next stranger you see.

They need it.

Respect.

Do unto others.

It's the right thing to do.

Always.

Consistently try your hardest.

Work hard.

Endure.

Turn pain into ways to help others.

It's OK to hurt.

Cry.

Search out funny things.

Joke and laugh.

LOL.

Sing even if you can't carry a tune.

Crank it up.

Jam.

Inspire people,

It feels good.

Trust.

You control your choices.

Every day.

Mood.

Not too much. Not too little.

Indulge yet be healthy.

Balance.

Don't waste another minute.

Enjoy time.

Maximize.

Don't have any regrets.

Go for it!

React.

IT'S A YES WEEK!

Yes, you can do it!

Yes, you will persevere.

Yes, you shall overcome.

Yes, to productivity.

Yes, to closing that deal.

Yes, to endurance.

Yes, to research and practice.

Yes, to winning.

Yes, to grit.

Yes. Yes. Yes.

Are you ready to rock this week?

Endurance-outwork the rest so you can reach success!

YOUR TRIBE BECOMES YOUR VIBE

The people you surround yourself with impact your attitude.

-Are they supportive?

-Do they encourage you?

-Would they pick you up if you were down?

-Do they make you want to be a better person?

-Do you smile and laugh when you are with them?

-Are they good for your health and well-being?

-Will they challenge you to think bigger? Do they push you to achieve more?

-Do they have faith in the same things you believe in?

-Would you do the same for them?

Evaluate your sphere of influence and make sure you are where you want to be.

PURPOSE

Find your purpose and hold on... because it will make you:

-Fight harder.

-Live larger.

-Be bolder.

-Stand taller.

-Speak louder.

-Climb mountains.

-Overcome hurdles.

Prepare your mind for great things ahead. Clear your mind and allow changes to happen.

YOUR HEART

Your heart beats faster when a thrill awaits. Be awakened to feel the sensations.

Your heart skips a beat when it gets crushed. Be resilient to love again.

Your heart is filled with warmth when you are cared for. Be able to receive the thoughtfulness.

Your heart can't speak. Be ready to use your eyes to say what your heart can't communicate.

Your heart grows tired when it gets hurt. Be relentless in strengthening it.

Your heart smiles when you find joy. Be able to learn from mistakes and process the pain.

Your heart is red because it burns with emotions. Be perfectly imperfect and accept your flaws.

Your heart struggles when difficult times arise. Be steadfast in your faith to overcome trials.

Your heart can feel lonely if you let it. Be bold to try new things and surround yourself with those who want to be in your presence.

Your heart can grow as you find love. Be comfortable enough to love yourself so you can do good for others.

Your heart beats slowly when you are nearing the end. Be proud of the legacy you leave, as you have made your mark. (Love you, Grandma)

ROLLING DOUBLES

You have a 16.7% probability of rolling doubles with 2 fair six-sided dice. Research concludes that 21.5% of startups fail in the first year, 30% in the second year, 50% in the fifth year, and 70% in their 10th year.

Reasons include lack of money, being in the wrong market, lack of research, bad partnerships, ineffective marketing, and not being an expert in the industry.

The good news is that you can succeed if you don't give up.

-Research-Host focus groups to test your concept. Then, work towards "proof of concept."

-Don't give up. Hard times will make you want to throw in the towel. Push through them.

-Accept a little luck if it comes your way. Even the most successful owners say they needed a little luck in being at the right place at the right time.

-Believe in your skills, but keep sharpening them.

-Love it. To have enough determination to fight through the rough patches, you have to love it.

-Do whatever it takes. If that means working two jobs to pay your bills while still maintaining your company, then determine if you believe in it enough to build it. Then, fight for what you believe in.

Doubles are hard to roll. But how sweet it will be when you get on a winning streak by betting on yourself.

EMBRACE THE CLIMB

Inventors: Keep inventing.

Athletes: Keep training.

Parents: Keep parenting.

Leaders: Keep leading.

Owners: Keep owning.

Influencers: Keep influencing.

There will be rough terrain. There will be peaks and valleys. And quite honestly, there will be times when you buckle down and cry. When it gets the steepest, you'll need to dig the deepest.

You can. You will.

PURPOSE

It's there. It's inside you. You may not know it yet, but it is! Everyone has a purpose, a reason for going beyond what he/she thinks they are capable of.

How did I find my purpose? I prayed for God to use me for his will and not my own. I was blessed to have my three amazing sons, which was and will always be my #1 purpose.

In 2012, my outlook on life changed when I met kids who were battling cancer. I was open to receiving and was blessed to meet other people's kids, who opened my eyes. That's how my book idea began. Then, hard work, relentless pursuit to impact, and hard work. Tears mixed with laughs. Failures and successes.

Open your mind to find your purpose. Allow your heart to beat for something outside of your inner circle. Find that thing you didn't think you were capable of. That thing you've been putting off because you are too busy. That thing that could make an impact on the world. That thing that could change lives. That thing that you were meant to do.

Find your purpose and hold on... because it will make you:

-Fight harder.

-Live larger.

-Be bolder.

-Stand taller.

-Speak louder.

-Climb mountains.

-Overcome hurdles.

Prepare your mind for great things ahead. Clear your mind and allow changes to happen.

THANK YOU

We should all say it more.

Thank you for your messages. I read every single one. I create and control my own content. I build my own connections. It's important for me to always be grateful to those of you who view it. I appreciate your support.

A few ways to say THANK YOU:

-Remember to say it verbally.

-Remind your employees to follow suit. If you are telling them, they will likely tell others.

-Board meetings—have a recognition time set aside in your agenda.

-Host a client appreciation party.

-Set aside one day a week to be your "give thanks" hour and do it your way.

-Give gifts, gas cards, meals, etc.

-Take time to teach them. Sometimes, people just want to soak in your knowledge.

WORK SMARTER & HARDER

Hard work is rolling up your sleeves and doing whatever it takes to get the job done.

Sweat—Don't be afraid to get your hands in the dirt. As a leader, we need to understand every detail about how our operation works and appreciate those who help get the work done.

Tears—Yes, it might require really hard times that may make you cry. It's fine. A few tears mean that you want it BAD. You are passionate.

Heart—If you are only working for a paycheck, you could reach burnout. I'd like to challenge you to find what makes your heart beat faster. Then, your job becomes more meaningful.

Grit—Get after it! Get things done. Stop thinking about options. Start implementing.

Stamina—In order to sustain results, you need consistent efforts from everyone around you. Training and motivation help propel productivity.

Even if you are the sharpest tool in the shed, hard work is essential to get to the top.

-Put in the time.

-Don't throw in the towel too early.

-Create a solid strategy.

-Broaden your circle.

-Make decisions.

-Understand your strengths & weaknesses.

Then, go to Jellystone and get your pic-a-nic basket!

WILL YOU ACCEPT MY FINAL ROSE?

Today, I want to talk to you about ACCEPTANCE. Do you accept the fact that you were created for something remarkable? Do you think you are capable of delivering on the things you were meant to do? Do you truly believe that you can do hard things? Do you accept yourself as you are, or do you want someone else's life? Do you settle in your relationships because you don't think you are good enough? Do you stay content with your job, or do you strive for that next promotion?

Life isn't a cakewalk. There are heartbreaks, losses, struggles, mistakes, accidents, trials, and just downright hard stuff.

Good news! I'm offering you my final rose today because I believe every person has a purpose.

You see... if you take this advice (my rose), you might just find happiness.

-BE OPEN to believing that you have a reason for being here.

-BE OPEN to forgiving yourself for past mistakes.

-BE OPEN to figuring out what it is that you were put on earth to do.

-BE OPEN to listening to those who are cheering you on.

-BE OPEN to living your life... flaws & all.

-BE OPEN to accomplishing things that you thought were impossible.

My final rose is about loving yourself so that you can accomplish your goals and find your purpose.

On an airplane, you are instructed to put your mask on first so you can help others when they need help.

Similarly, I'm encouraging you to love yourself so you can have the strength to help others in business and in life.

OVERCOMING OBSTACLES

We all get stuck at times. We have used all of our brainpower on a project, and our creative juices stop flowing. We all have ups and downs. Hardships seem to hit us when we aren't expecting them.

If you get stuck, try these things:

1-Play music, move, and groove.

2-Get outside.

3-Ask for help.

4-Accept support.

5-Listen to a positive speaker on an unrelated topic to take your mind off of the thing you are stuck on.

You need fresh air, fun, and a well-deserved break! Then, spin around to a brighter future. Music calms. Nature soothes. Fun conquers.

Stuff happens. Let's overcome it together, one day at a time.

NO EXCUSES!

Are you the one who makes up excuses whenever something goes wrong, or are you the one who owns up to mistakes, figures out solutions, and moves forward?

Mistakes are bound to happen.

Let's start trying this when they do:

-Own it.

-Figure out a remedy.

-Forgive yourself.

-Seek outside help, find mentors, and surround yourself with a supportive network.

-Hit the reset button and keep trying.

-Push through it, knowing there is something brighter, Iggy, around the corner.

Let's go!!! Bye-bye excuses. Hello, opportunities!!!

Earn it!

Hey! We aren't entitled to a window seat on an airplane if we don't reserve it in advance.

We aren't entitled to a promotion if we don't put in the work and earn it.

We aren't entitled to cut in line at amusement parks or anywhere.

We aren't entitled to the best of what's offered.

We earn it.

We work for it.

We put in the time and effort.

We strive for more.

We build our own relationships.

We choose how to spend our time, which sometimes equates to productivity and positive results.

We choose how we treat others, which can result in friendships and genuine relationships.

Nothing should be "expected."

Everything should be asked for or earned.

Then, show gratitude and respect for those around you once you receive good things.

There's only one YOU. Make sure people remember you for earning what you achieve and giving back once you receive.

VALUE CHAMPION

Are you a salesperson or a value champion?

Nearly every job requires some type of sales, so it's good to know how to do it effectively. I'd like to encourage you to become a champion of providing value instead of selling your product or service.

I believe there are a few keys to being a value champion:

1-Add value—Create something your customer truly needs that will help them grow their business, better their life, increase their productivity, or fulfill a need that makes them happier.

2-Solve problems—Develop a product or service that solves a problem that your customer has. Always think about the solution that can benefit others.

3-Fill a void—Step up and fill in a gap that hasn't been discovered yet. Don't be afraid to invent something new.

4-Treat them right—Everyone wants to be treated with respect. No one wants to be sold to. Understand the difference between a hard sell that is self-focused and a strategy where you genuinely care about the other person's life and results.

If someone asks you if you are a salesperson, your response can now be, "I'm a value champion. I provide solutions and add value to other people's lives and business because it's the right thing to do."

Simple, yet effective. Try it.

VIVA LAS VEGAS

In Vegas, the odds are against you. In business, you might feel like the odds are against you, but they aren't. Each person is born with specific qualities. At various stages of our lives, many factors come into play that determine our productivity levels. Education helps sharpen skills. Real-life experiences aid in the amount of knowledge we acquire over time. Personality and attitude are critical in order to improve. And luck. Yes, luck. At times, being in the right place at the right time is important. If you become a problem solver instead of a fear instigator, you might open the doors for a brilliant mind to be unleashed. I can't even imagine how many solutions for major problems went right into the grave with someone who was just too afraid to step out of their comfort zone to share or take action on it.

UNLEASH BRILLIANCE

1-If you are a decision-maker, allow others to step up and be vocal.

2-Reward great ideas.

3-If you run a business, expect ideas from all levels of staff.

4-If you are the idea person, step up and be vocal.

5-If one idea doesn't fly, try another...and another...

In order to change your odds in business and in life, you must believe in yourself, understand your worth, and have a relentless pursuit of making a difference.

If you believe the odds are with you, they can be.

STEP INTO THE RING

Business professionals need to have the same type of mindset as a boxer getting ready to step into the ring. Get ready to approach each day with your best hook, jab, and cross. It takes a variety of punches to beat your opponents.

It is also good to balance the serious with a little fun to keep the days interesting.

-Practice. Research your opponent.

-Prepare. Create your business plan

-Train. Keep your mindset strong and bold to make decisions.

-Execute. Sell. Build relationships.

-Fight.

-Use every ounce of your power to fight for your job, your business, and your passion.

-Balance. Add a little fun to the mix.

Toughen up. Step into the ring every single day, ready to battle! After the battle, laugh...learn, and impact lives.

BROAD SHOULDERS

In business and in life, you need to have broad shoulders to push through challenging times. The ability to accept criticism and take responsibility is important.

Try these alternatives when someone takes issue with you or your work:

-Realize that those who lash out may have their own problems they are dealing with.

-Be big enough to accept it when you are wrong.

-When you are right, stand up for yourself.

-Communicate and listen to what others say without thinking of your response while they are talking.

-Own your mistakes, apologize, and find ways to become better.

-Forgive the person who brought it to your attention, and be respectful that they thought enough of you to tell you.

-Stay humble, be grateful, and work harder.

-Allow QB Darla to help you improve your positive mindset playbook.

SMACKDOWN

When our business associates or friends fall, help them back up.

When people post good content, look for ways to support them.

When businesses grow, cheer them on.

When underdogs overcome hurdles, be proud of them.

When humans struggle, listen to their needs.

When leaders win, celebrate with them.

No jealousy. No hidden agenda. No ego. No bad vibes.

Everyone needs to surround themselves with people who will build them up.

Be the change agent. Set the trend of unconditional support without expecting paybacks. Make it cool to give accolades instead of negativity, high fives instead of complaints, fist bumps instead of talking behind backs, and joy instead of jealousy.

If you fall, you are not alone. There are people who want to help you rebound. So... when you get back up and put the smackdown on, it's your turn to help someone else succeed.

KICK IT UP A NOTCH

● If you think you're doing everything right, you can always kick it up a notch!

● If you think you are getting by fine, you can always put in a little more effort. Add hot sauce!

● If you think you have all the right ingredients (people in place), you can always use an outside opinion to offer new ideas.

● If you get in a rut, there's always a way out. Build a solid foundation, and it will eventually light.

Kick it up a notch, my friends.

Cheers to cooking up new business ideas to keep it fresh!

RODEO CLOWNS

Have you ever been to a rodeo? I was traveling in Texas and decided on a whim to go to my first rodeo. I hopped on a train and attended the Houston Rodeo by myself. I enjoyed the food, the trade show, and the entire rodeo experience. Bull riding was my favorite, even though I cringed several times as the rider was thrown off, flying into the air and then scurrying out of the bull's way. One guy was kicked... ouch! The train ride home was terrifying. That's another whole story, and why I keep my mom up at night when I travel.

The rodeo clowns have a job to do. They are to distract the bull so the cowboy doesn't get injured. They do this by waving their red flag and acting crazy so the mean bull will come after them instead of the rider.

The next time you complain about your job, think twice about it. Would you rather stare down the face of a 1600 lb. raging bull? Not me. My job as an entrepreneur just got a whole lot better.

Embrace the good.

No complaining.

Weather the storms.

Take risks, but avoid the bull when you fall. Get back up. Thank the rodeo clown (those who have your back).

Look at the bright side. You don't have a red flag as part of your work attire.

MILLION BUCKS

Your mindset is powerful. If you have confidence, you can accomplish anything. You can feel like a million bucks no matter what you wear, who you know, what house you live in, or what kind of car you drive.

Confidence is the feeling or belief that one can rely on someone or something.

First, believe in yourself. You have abilities that likely go beyond what you think you are capable of. Allow yourself to be inspired by yourself. Yes, that's right. You might be surprised if you allow your heart to lead the way.

Second, trust yourself once you do your research and create a plan.

Third, overcome insecurities and the feeling that you are inadequate.

Lastly, take action. Make things happen.

Strive for greatness in your own way! And remember... don't just dress to impress... dress to accomplish tasks, lead others, and make an impact!

LET'S GO TO MARS

When you think something is impossible, it isn't. It just hasn't been done yet. Guess what? You could be the first at something great. You could change the world. You could make things better than they were before you were born.

Nearly everything that you touch has been started from scratch. Many new ideas have been sketched on a napkin before the manufacturing process started. Many great inventors are among us, and one of them could be YOU!

How to get an idea from a napkin onto a boardroom table:

-Hire an attorney, conduct an initial patent search, and then file your application.

-Create a business plan and pitch deck.

-Identify the competition.

-Determine the need, target audience, and the problem it solves.

-Secure investors if necessary.

-Envision your products to change lives.

-Take action and see it through to the finish line.

-Go to Mars! Make it a reality.

-Find a "QB" to get things done so you won't sit on it and never see it through.

-Believe in it.

-Surround yourself with smart people.

-Identify reputable partners for manufacturing, design, and development.

-Be confident.

TODAY IS THE DAY YOU CATCH MY PASS!

I'd like for you to raise up your hands and get ready to catch this touchdown pass I'm throwing to you. Put your eye black on and get ready for battle.

Today is the day you RISE UP and start taking steps to prepare for your future.

Today is the day you decide to take on new tasks that you've always put off.

Today is the day you throw away past routines and start new ones.

Today is the day you forgive and let the past go.

Today is the day you start fresh with new ideas to propel you forward.

Today is the day you outwork, outsmart, and outshine your competition.

Today is the day you allow your passion to fuel your purpose.

Today is the day you reach out your arms and catch my pass to score your own touchdown in business and in life!

Today. Not tomorrow. Not next week. Not next year. TODAY.

WALK THE WALK

Talk the talk. Be authentic. Take action. Have fun!

I like to do random activities each workday to keep life interesting. Each person needs to think about their own interests, but here are a few things that I do on any given day to keep a good work/life balance:

-Workout

-Sing

-Dance

-Enjoy nature/scenery outdoors

-Go to a new restaurant

-Control my own content

-Help someone with a business question

-Send 5 encouraging messages to people who need encouragement

-Talk to my parents, kids, sister, or family members

-Send a funny GIF to someone

-Tell a funny story

-Plan a trip

-Mess up

-Repair what I mess up

-Surprise someone

-Small acts of goodness

-Trip on something (I move too fast)

-Admit that I don't get jokes

-Organize something

-Learn something new

-Drive too fast

-Burn what I cook, throw it out, and call Door Dash

-Listen to good live music

-See what's up on social media (only look at the positive vibes)

-Pray

-Give

-Write something impactful

-Tell someone they are special

-Thank a mentor

You don't necessarily need to make a list. Just give some thought to what makes you happy. What helps you break up your day? What do you enjoy that would make your work more enjoyable... therefore more productive. Stay true to YOU.

Make it FUN!

MOVE MOUNTAINS

I've always taken risks. Roller coasters, watching TV on my head, riding four-wheelers, playing sports, trying anything adventurous, and starting new businesses. Look, ma...no hands! Entrepreneurship is not an easy road. It's full of peaks and valleys.

I worked in marketing and advertising most of my life, moving up the ranks in each company I worked for by putting in extra hours and working hard.

I wasn't afraid to fail because I knew that I would work harder the next time to succeed.

Mountaineers get to the peak and enjoy the view. But did you know that it's dangerous coming back down, and some don't make it?

They face hazards such as the environment, weather, dangerous terrain, and equipment failure.

Things they can do to prepare for the ascent and descent (and these relate to business as well):

-Plan ahead

-Check the weather

-Train

-Research

-Create a roadmap

-Sharpen your skills

-Pack the right tools/gear

-Have the right mindset

Climb to the top! Enjoy the view. Then, make sure you are prepared for avalanches. Remember to stay focused until you get all the way back to safety.

GOALS

Goals are great, but the magic happens when your goals become reality. You must be dedicated to turning your ideas into viable projects.

I'll give you one example that I am working towards.

I set a goal of developing a children's storybook kit to give families a new adventure during the holidays. I didn't write it down as a goal. I just knew I wanted to accomplish it to make an impact and teach kids about goodness.

Here's how I personally make things happen:

-I decided to do it.

-I brainstormed the concept.

-I wrote the story.

-I created the character and hired an illustrator to draw him.

-I found a manufacturer for the book, plush, and accessories by contacting one of my mentors whom I've built a relationship with.

-I hustled to earn money so I could afford to build out 10 prototypes.

-I started networking and listed 10 publishers I'm going to pitch it to.

-I am now in the process of creating 10 completed kits to ship to the publishers to see if they want to adopt my creation.

-I have a plan A and a plan B already in the works to make it happen. Plan A is to find a publisher. Plan B is to do it myself.

-I've visualized my creation in the hands of children doing good deeds and documenting their journey during the holidays.

You see... having goals is only the first part of the plan. Taking action on your goals is what makes the magic happen.

Now, go make your own magic happen in your own way for your own reasons. Set goals, but then get them done!

Stay tuned to see if my idea becomes a reality. Do you think it will?

THINK TWICE

Think twice before you leave your shopping cart anywhere except where it belongs.

Think twice before you expect someone else to pick up your trash.

Think twice before you post something degrading or decisive on social media.

Think twice before you make a mistake and refuse to own up to it.

Think twice before you look outwardly for someone else to fix your flaws.

Think twice before you give up.

Think twice before you become complacent with the status quo.

Think twice before you blame someone else without knowing all the facts.

Think twice before you stop believing in yourself.

You've got this! Now, think twice about going for it and do it!

If you're too big to do the small things, you might be too small to do the big things.

REACH YOUR POTENTIAL

In life, there are thresholds we face. Do you push harder to overcome the latent abilities within you that lead to future success, or do you ignore what lies ahead of you? Our choices determine whether we maximize our talents in business and life. Reach your potential! Go beyond what you think you can or should do each day.

How?

-When you get up each day, think about what you need to accomplish. Write them down. Then, do those things... plus 3 more!

-Dream bigger and think about the things you want, the reasons why you want to succeed, and the impact you will make.

-Give yourself a little slack. If you are too hard on yourself, you'll buckle. Forgive yourself daily and get back on your tasks the following day. Everyone has "off" days.

-Realize your true potential by listening to what other people tell you (the ones who believe in you).

-Continually educate yourself on new things, be open to different ways of accomplishing things, and learn from mistakes.

-Exceed the magnitude or intensity of each project so that results can be manifested.

I'm cheering for you to reach your potential! It's a process. Now is the time to start believing that you can do it! It starts and ends with your choices.

Be determined

If you are determined, you won't:

-allow distractions

-give up

-blame others

-expect others to do your work for you

-let negative people deter you

If you are determined, you will:

-face every gut-wrenching decision with the will to get through it

-dig deeper than every competitor -find solutions to problems

-think outside and around the box

-make the calls even when you don't feel like it

-see the future with results that are going to happen

You may question things. You may get scared. You may doubt yourself. You may even want to quit... But YOU DON'T.

Let me say that again...You don't QUIT.

And that, my friends, is what creates winners.

MADE FROM SCRATCH

When you start a business from scratch, it's rewarding. I didn't have a lot of money to start with back in 2011. $20,000 to be exact. I didn't know a lot about publishing or licensing deals. I dug in and learned everything by doing research, talking to smart people, teaching myself, and working hard. I believed in my products and how they would impact lives. I saw how they made kids smile, and that inspired me to want to accomplish more.

I made mistakes. I struggled. I overcame hurdles. I cried. I laughed.

I learned and fine-tuned my strategies, created more efficient systems, developed lower-risk manufacturing scenarios, and tapped into my resources to keep going full steam ahead.

I listened to mentors. I valued their opinions and put their suggestions into action.

I'm imperfect. I don't allow past mistakes or fear to keep me from moving forward and taking chances.

I'm not 'self-made.' I'm self "in the making." That means "in progress." Thanks for allowing me to step into your lives for brief moments on social media and offer encouragement, smiles, and motivation.

Today, I encourage you to take some chances. Don't allow mistakes or fear to keep you from reaching high. REACH!

STAY HUNGRY

You know that feeling in your stomach when you haven't eaten for hours? It starts to growl. It swirls around, making weird noises. You might feel light-headed. Then, you eat. You get full. But...are you satisfied?

In business, it's so important to STAY HUNGRY!

-Be determined to get results.

-Outpace your competitors.

-Stay motivated each day to work hard.

-Fight off complacency. Get out of the rut.

-Don't settle.

-Allow ambition to fuel you.

If you stay hungry, you aren't allowing your stomach or your soul to feel satisfied. You are yearning for more. You start thinking bigger. You start believing and planning for big opportunities to become real.

MOMENTS

Don't blink. The moments in your life will fly by. Your kids will grow up. Your parents will grow old. You may experience loss. You will see changes that you never thought would happen.

Cherish every single moment. You get the gift of life. The gift of 365 days a year, 8760 hours, or 529,949.2 minutes. Make every second count.

Hard work wins.

Are you retired? Be proud.

Are you employed? Be proud.

Do you own a business, or are you self-employed? Be proud.

Are you starting over? Be proud.

Whatever stage you are at, be proud if you are working hard and putting in the effort it takes to make improvements. Visualize results, then roll up your sleeves to make it happen.

You are Necessary

Needed to make the world a better place.

Essential to others around you.

Crafted to be unique.

Existing to do great things.

Special in your own way.

Superstar in the making.

Achieve your goals and dreams.

Require self-love and commitment.

YOU are necessary for all the right reasons. Now, go take action to make the world a better place.

SELF-ASSESSMENT

Instead of blaming others, look in the mirror first. Ask yourself if you have exhausted all efforts to help the situation. Then, self-reflect.

Try these tips:

1- Be slow to judge and quick to help.

2- Think about all of the ways you can be a part of the solution instead of the problem.

3- On social media, post positive content that does good. Avoid hurtful, divisive posts.

4- If you need to vent, do it in private with your inner circle of trusted friends or with a professional.

5- Spend more time in self-reflection. Jot down 10 things you need to work on, then take action.

6- Appreciate your strengths and use them wisely.

7- Recognize your flaws, and don't be too proud to make adjustments.

8- Believe in your abilities and use them for good.

9- Open your heart to forgive others.

10- Be bold, but be compassionate.

11- Realize that you can't win all the time. We all lose sometimes, but that doesn't mean you have to give up. Keep working towards your goals.

Stand up for what you believe in, but be willing to continue to do the right things: Love people, be kind, be peaceful, find solutions, strive for happiness, and make the world a better place for generations to come.

MOOOOOD

What changes your mood? My hope is that you will read this and start thinking positively.

Your mood is set by you the moment you roll out of bed. Here are a few tips on controlling your mood:

1- Control it so it doesn't control you. Remind yourself that everything is going to be OK. Time heals.

2- Take action to roll out of bed on the right side. The right side is +. The wrong side is -.

3- Play your favorite songs, think happy thoughts, get outside, and be thankful for the small things.

4- Throughout your day, try to make giving back or being nice to others a priority.

5- Enjoy life knowing that every second counts to make an impact on those around you.

6- Do goofy things, watch funny movies, talk to positive people, and watch uplifting videos. Laugh often.

7- Mooooo-ve over bacon. Try eating healthy and exercising.

8- Remember that the better mood you are in, the more productive your day will be.

10- No matter how hard life gets, stay positive and keep trying hard to change it for the better. One day at a time. Persistence pays off.

HERO

Who is your hero?

My heroes are the kids who are battling a disease, an illness, an injury, or a hardship. It's the Braxtons, Averys, Violets, and Avas who have bravely battled leukemia. It's the Ryan, Eli, Hunter, Carson, Thomas, and many others who have gained their wings. It's the Gideons who are fighting and loving people throughout their journey. It is the Natalie and Carson who are recovering from accidents. It's the kids who have been bullied, abused, or who haven't eaten a meal in three days. My heroes haven't quite experienced jobs, break-ups, or adult struggles, but they have fought, loved, laughed, given back, and had a positive attitude doing it. They have cheered their peers on. They have experienced a deep relationship with God and others that we may never see.

Today, I want to encourage you to cheer others on. There is no room for jealousy and inferiority in a world that needs to be built back up. There is a need for love, support, kindness, humility, and words of encouragement.

Let's keep our feeds uplifting over the next 15 days. Take time to identify yourself heroes and let them know that they inspire you.

A SMILE IS FREE

When someone makes you happy, smile at them.

When someone makes you proud, smile at them.

When someone makes you laugh, smile at them.

When someone is sad, be there for them.

When someone is hurting, be there for them.

When someone accomplishes something, cheer them on.

When someone has a great day, be happy for them.

Your gift of a smile will brighten someone's day. I challenge you to turn your mood into a gift to offer someone over the next few weeks.

People often think that buying gifts is an important part of the holidays. I think the simple things are the key. A smile is free. Listening is free. Being present in the moment is free. Making someone feel proud is free.

Do you accept this challenge? It's free.

TAKE A DEEP BREATH

If you make a mistake, take a deep breath. A lot of us make them.

If you fail, take a deep breath. A lot of us do it at some point in our lives.

If you have been embarrassed, take a deep breath. A lot of us have been.

If you have been uncomfortable, take a deep breath, as most of us have squirmed before.

If you have made a fool out of yourself, take a deep breath. A lot of us have done that.

Those deep breaths will calm your soul if you realize that you aren't alone in this imperfect world. Forgive yourself.

Quit beating yourself up for mistakes and imperfections. We are all imperfect. Just learn and keep working towards your goals.

LIKKITY-SPLIT

When you find your passion, things become more clear. You tend to work harder, build faster, and fight relentlessly.

When you find your passion, things become more prioritized. You tend to focus, not take no for an answer, and strive for bigger goals.

When you allow your passion to drive your purpose, things seem to be more fun. You tend to have less stress, less anxiety, and less sadness.

When you realize that life is better when you serve others in some capacity, things seem to happen naturally. You tend to create happiness for those around you and not sweat the small stuff, and worry about your own imperfections.

Find your passion likkity-split. You'll start to get up each day and work harder for your end results. Chop chop...there's no better time than the present. People say they can't wait until 2020 is over.

I'd like to encourage you to make the most out of every single day from here forward. Although life can throw you curves and be challenging, let's learn from those struggles to become better humans in order to impact those around us.

We are strong. Together, we can accomplish great things for those we love and those strangers who may need a lift.

TOUCHDOWN

It's 4th & 10 with 10 left on the clock. You are down by 4. You are on your 15-yard line. Fans are going crazy! Will you run the ball or throw it? If your business was on the line, what would you do to score a touchdown? If something in your life was going wrong, would you throw in the towel or dig in and go for the touchdown?

It doesn't matter if you run or pass. The important thing is that you don't give up. You make that call. You prepare for moments like this. You give your team the tools they need to be confident in their choices. You do your research. You put your best team on the field or in the boardroom.

-Call the play with confidence so your team believes in it.

-Have faith in your team and surround yourself with those who will cheer you on to score big.

-Deal with the results, knowing you gave it your best shot.

-Leave it all on the field. Grit wins in business and in life.

-If you lose, keep trying.

-If you win, give thanks and count your blessings. Give back.

It takes a team, even if you feel alone in your business or life at times. Even the best QBs in the league need support and guidance. Enjoy Thanksgiving and give thanks. Then, get ready to score your own touchdowns in business and in life!

ADAPT. FIND SOLUTIONS. RE-CHARGE

Finish these sentences first, thinking about your family, then about your work, dreams, and future goals.

I feel happy when...

I feel thankful for...

I feel grateful for...

I feel lucky when...

We should recognize our blessings and dig deep to see the good in life.

I'd like to challenge you to do four things:

1- Adapt to change. If you have lost a job or had a career change, take this opportunity to educate yourself and be open to new opportunities. Don't give up because the right thing may be just around the corner. If you are struggling with uncertainty, surround yourself with positive people and messages to help build your self-esteem.

2- Work hard to find solutions to problems. In all situations, try to think about each problem one at a time. Reflect on it and look inwardly first. Once you do that, think through three potential solutions to be the bigger person and make things right. Put pride aside and humble yourself to say you are sorry, forgive someone, or offer solutions that involve you helping others.

3- Take time to re-focus, recharge, and reinvent yourself. Grab blank sheets of paper and go old school. Write down your goals, purpose, and vision. Think ahead and write down the things you want to buy, accomplish, donate, and succeed at.

4- With every idea, there needs to be ACTION. Make it happen.

I am cheering for you to WIN-WIN-WIN. Don't be too hard on yourself if m

KEEP SWINGING

Hank Aaron played 21 seasons for the Milwaukee and Atlanta Braves and then two seasons for the Milwaukee Brewers. He also held the MLB record for career home runs for 33 years.

He was once in a hitting slump, and he was asked by a teammate how he was going to come out of it. He said, "Oh, I called Mr. Stan Musial about it, and I'm coming out of it."

"What did Mr. Musial tell you to do?" asked the teammate.

He said, "Keep swinging." Shortly thereafter, his slump passed, and Henry ended with a .362 finish.

When we get down or when things aren't going the way we planned, we need to remember to KEEP SWINGING.

How can you keep swinging?

1- When life throws curveballs, step up to the plate and swing away.

2- When you face a slider, adapt and make adjustments to your stance.

3- Every player on the team has a purpose, even those who sit on the bench. Keep practicing, learning, and getting better. Help make your teammates better.

4- If you get in a life slump, remember that it is temporary.

5- Don't let fear of getting hit by a ball keep you from stepping up to the plate.

LITTLE HELPERS

Hummingbirds are more than just the smallest birds in the world. They play a crucial role in the environment as pollinators. They are little helpers.

I can relate. Standing 4'11, 3/4" and weighing in at 108 lbs, I love helping people. Small but mighty.

How can you help people?

1- Listen to them. Find out what their pains are. Ask them what makes them happy.

2- Make time for it. If you are the busiest person in the world, you can still make time to help others.

3- Do it. Pollinate the earth with smiles, good gestures, kind words, and actions of gratitude.

Fly away, little birdies. Sprinkle good deeds out there in the world.

BE STRONG

In all things you do, do them with conviction. Believe in yourself. You have the ability to research, work hard, and control your choices. If you make a choice that turns out bad, look in the mirror to reflect on how you can improve and move forward.

Be Bold

In all things you do, be powerful. You were made for a purpose, and that should be enough to sustain any self-doubt. If you can make decisions, you will get things done. If procrastination has a grip on you, change your routine and create an action plan.

Be a Light

In all things you do, have compassion for those around you. Always consider how your words and actions will impact others around you. As people hurt, help them heal. As they celebrate, toast to their success. Change makes us better.

In all situations, be a light that shines positivity. Offer a high-five, a smile, or a kind gesture.

Hop out of your comfort zone.

If I stayed in my comfort zone, I would not have cashed in my savings and started a business.

If I stayed in my comfort zone, I would not have been able to sell $1.4M in activity books.

If I stayed in my comfort zone, I would have never impacted sick kids' lives who needed someone to love them.

If I stayed in my comfort zone, I could not have made the hard decisions to adapt in my business.

If I stayed in my comfort zone, I would have never been brave enough to allow my passion to drive my purpose.

If you stay comfortable, how will you know what you can accomplish? How will you impact lives? How will you go beyond what you think you can do?

Surround yourself with great mentors who push you beyond your comfort zone! Get uncomfortable and strive for more! It's not always easy. It's hard. But hard things make us more resilient.

FEAR IS NOT A FACTOR

We live in a world of ups and downs, twists and turns, peaks and valleys.

Let's try these few things to keep a positive mindset today:

-Monitor what comes in so we can control what comes out.

-Include nature & exercise in our day.

-Detox from negativity, yet be compassionate and prayerful for those impacted in these days of turmoil.

-Learn from our own mistakes so we become better for those around us.

-Allow fear to give us patience, but not deter us from what we think is right.

-Let go of our past failures and start building on our future successes.

-Love others and allow that love to shine in our darkest moments.

-Rally around each other to make the world a better place.

Fear is not a factor when it comes to following our passions to impact the world.

BE NICE

When tragedy strikes, we should be nice to one another.

If you are nice, you are looking at yourself first and making sure that you are making this world a better place.

If you are nice, you are teaching your kids to include everyone.

If you are nice, you are complimenting others in the workplace, at the drive-thru, at the grocery, in the mall, at church, or wherever you go.

If you are nice, you are posting encouraging thoughts to help people, not hurt people.

If you are nice, you are not talking smack behind someone's back.

If you are nice, you are looking for the good in someone, even if they can't see it in themselves.

If you are nice, your heart is filled with love for humankind. Your words and actions can display that love.

If you are nice, you are delightful to be around.

Back to the basics. Be nice, everyone.

ROOTS

Tree roots serve several purposes. Not only do they anchor the tree and draw in nutrients and water from the soil, but tree roots also help stabilize the soil and prevent erosion. Feeder roots absorb surface water and minerals and are very efficient.

There are so many negative factors that can seep into our lives. Toxic relationships, job problems, negative people, sad stories, hard times, death, and many other issues tend to bring us down.

We need roots to stabilize us. In order to maintain a positive mindset, we need to consider the following:

1-Reflect on our past and appreciate where we came from.

2-Allow more positive people than negative people to provide nutrients to your soul.

3-Water yourself with good deeds, which also help others.

4-Absorb sunshine and explore nature.

5-Prevent erosion by fighting off any negative thoughts that try to creep into your brain.

Let's all take a deep breath today and get a hold of our thoughts. Look at the tree roots and think about these things that you can control. Your mindset sets the stage for your daily routine. Make it as great as it can be.

PAINS=LESSONS YOU OVERCOME

What are you afraid of?

Heartbreak?

Losing a job?

Your boss, co-workers?

A virus?

Marriage?

Being alone?

Snakes, mice, spiders?

Flying, skydiving, heights?

Caves, elevators, confinement?

Water, ocean, sharks?

Scary movies?

Loved ones' safety?

Starting something new? A new business? New job? New relationship?

Bridges, driving, other people's driving?

Death?

Losing your phone, not having social media?

Yourself? Your mind? Your thoughts?

Everyone has their own way of coping. There is a threshold of pain that we tend to be able to handle. Then, a tragedy happens, and we say things like, "This really makes me appreciate what I have." Why does it take a tragedy to make us realize that we deserve happiness? Why can't we turn our fears into challenges that we can overcome if we choose to do so? Everyone has a finite number of days to live, to impact others, to love, and to enjoy life. When I go through painful situations, I have a talk with myself. I say, "Hard times are temporary. There is a greater plan that I'm not seeing just yet. God is in control, and I'm here to do the work using my talents. I am worthy of happiness. I'm OK with circumstances that are out of my control."

Turn your pain into lessons that you give yourself the power to overcome! Live deliberately.

LOVE YOURSELF

If you love yourself and your purpose in life, you don't need other people to make you happy. You will glow with happiness that others will gravitate towards because you are just fine with your imperfections.

It's time for you to start loving yourself. Start believing in your talents. If a human thinks that another human is going to complete them, they may be disappointed. Relationships are tricky. Business is hard. Life is a roller coaster. If you are content with who God designed you to be, you will allow your flaws to keep you humble but proud. There's nothing wrong with saying these things:

"I've got this!"

"I can do it!"

"I'm imperfect but perfectly made."

"I'm OK being alone."

"I'm going to control the things I can control and let go of the things I can't."

"I'm not giving up."

"I'm going to reach my goals."

"I am special and unique."

"I'm going to kick @ss today."

"I can do hard things."

"I will learn from the bad and make it good."

"I will not let others deter me, distract me, or bring me down because I'm in charge of myself."

"I'm stronger today than I was yesterday."

Say these things out loud. Print them and put them on your bathroom mirror. Say them out loud every day. Believe them because today is the day you stand up and start loving yourself. Today is the day you gain strength from your own body. Today is the day your heart heals. Today is the day you take care of yourself so that you can love others in a way that they deserve to be loved. One step at a time. You will heal.

REACH BEYOND

The stars in Heaven shine down.

The sun's rays burn bright in the sky.

When you don't believe in goodness, reach up and grab onto a ray of hope.

Don't give up on faith or humanity.

There's always someone who needs you.

Someone dear to me once said, "It's never too late to change anything about ourselves. Maybe God has you right where you need to be to hear His voice and guidance." This, my friends, is the true measure of a man—one who forgives. One who has hurt and been hurt yet forgives. One who is deserving of the best that life has to offer. We all make mistakes, but let's try to wrap our arms around each other and show compassion for humankind.

We all strive for happiness. Let's give each other the gift of hope, courage, faith, and forgiveness. Shine bright for those around you, like the stars in the sky, and the rays of hope beaming down for us to be a reflection of.

BAGGAGE

We've all got some! Those stories to tell, those funny things we did growing up, those stupid decisions we made, the people we hurt, mistakes, a job we lost, hurdles we couldn't overcome, words we said...on and on and on...

Today, I encourage you to let it go. Your past is your past. Forgive yourself. Live to start right now to impact your future. Start doing the things you want to do, surrounding yourself with people who want to be in your life, helping others... whatever it is that you want to do.

If someone wants to be a part of your life, you'll know by their actions. If a business partner decides to bail... It's OK. Let them go like a beautiful butterfly coming out of its cocoon. If a plan doesn't work, it's OK. Find another blueprint for success. Move on. Adapt.

Your mindset from this day forward is going to be positive, not negative. Helpful, not hurtful. You are going to believe in yourself, your talents, your brain, and your fighting spirit.

Get rid of the baggage and start fresh today!

HERE & NOW

What are you waiting for? How much time do you have left to bless others with your God-given talents? Yes, you have them!

Start living. Start loving. Start giving.

Start a new venture. Start enjoying your job. Start being the best person you can be.

Why?

Well, why not?

-You never know how much your gifts can help someone else.

-You just need to stop underestimating how powerful you are.

-Stop comparing yourself to others and just own who you are.

Checkered Flag

♥🏁♥ May is typically race month in Indianapolis. Every year, my friends and I get excited to hear the engines, people watch, and enjoy the race festivities.

Things we can do when you get the yellow flag and things slow down:

-We can take a pit stop to get gas and new tires.

-We can fine-tune our business plans and pivot to a greater plan.

-We can talk to the crew chief to revamp our strategies so we get into a better pole position.

-We can clear our minds from clutter and distractions so we can focus on one lap at a time.

-We can work fast, knowing that every second counts in order for us to get back out on the oval track.

-We can maintain the will to win the checkered flag.

Ladies and gentlemen... start your engines! Let's get ready to race back into business & life!

Prepared, not perfect

Confident, yet humble.

Confidence comes from being prepared, not perfect.

How do you prepare?

-Do your homework.

-Study

-Take notes

-Ask questions

-Find mentors

-Be vulnerable

-Focus

-Make decisions

-Take action

-Take rejection and turn it into a positive

-Allow mistakes to humble you, not deter you.

-Think of the worst outcome and create a plan A, B, and C.

-Think of the best outcome and then dream a little bigger.

Humility enables us to share our vulnerable side. This enables us to listen to others and become better.

Be humble yet confident! You've got this!

Keep building for you and for those around you.

STAY ON TOP OF YOUR GAME

What are your end goals? Why do you want to reach the top? Who will help you get there? Will you play an easy or tough course?

If you are an overachiever, come on a journey with me to reach higher than the loftiest goal you have set. Write down your goals and leave space for one more at the very top. That goal is going to be something that you don't think you can hit, but others around you think you can.

Stand up. Reach as high as you can. If that's what you desire, let's do this!

Then, get ready to reach even higher. Climb to the top with me. I'll be here to help you get there. I'll encourage you so you start believing in yourself. I'll push you up the hill so you can see the flag.

With focus and determination, the toughest things are possible.

If you hit your ball into the rough, you might just need to adjust your swing.

Bunkers are there to distract us. As much as we try to avoid them, we're going to need to pull out our sand wedge eventually.

You might combine your belief and skill to hit a hole-in-one! If you don't think you can, the chances are reduced. So why not believe in your capabilities? What do you have to lose?

I'll tell you. Here's what you have to lose:

-You have one life. There are only so many days to get things done.

-You will not succeed if you don't try.

-You could lose your chance to build a legacy for those to follow.

-You can't give back to make the world a better place if you don't try.

Believe in your talents. They were given to you for a reason.

Stay on top of your game.

SIMPLE MANNERS

Life is difficult enough with the challenges we all face. If we could remember these simple manners, we could do our part to make it a happier place to live and work.

1- Say please and thank you often. When you say it, mean it.

2- Do what you say. Say what you mean.

3- Forgive with a willingness to heal.

4- Treat others as you would like to be treated.

5- Allow your heart to be happy when others win.

6- Have fun.

7- Let yourself be human and learn to love who you are.

8- Give back.

9- Love your neighbor, honor your parents, and respect your elders.

10- Strive to be the best you can be, but always help others to succeed with you.

Fire ant video-blast from the past, but worth showing again.

AUTHENTICITY

I love just being real. Real is more fun. It's less stressful being authentic because it's easier to be who you are instead of faking someone you aspire to be. If we are content with our imperfections, life becomes more enjoyable.

Creating content every day is not that hard for me because I talk about real life. Everyone, including me, has challenges.

The most famous people in the world have problems. But yet, society still looks up to them as if they are untouchable.

Real=Mistakes

Real=Vulnerable

Real=Success

Real=Emotions

Real=Genuine

Real=Funny

Real=Relatable

When I film my motivational videos, I often times post the ones I mess up on because that's "real life."

There was one that I posted last year when I was sitting in a bed of fire ants. Ouch! I made fun of myself and learned to watch where I sat.

As we think about our lives, jobs, and businesses today... let's be REAL. Be proud of who you are, with flaws and all.

PUZZLES & HEARTS

Puzzles are complex.

They are hard to figure out.

So many sizes, shapes, and colors.

It takes time to identify where the pieces go. It's a process.

Life is complex.

At times, it is hard to figure out.

So many sizes, shapes, and colors.

It takes time to figure out some of the challenges we are faced with. It's a process.

To solve the puzzle, let's talk about your heart. Your heart rate, or pulse, is the number of times your heart beats per minute. If you're sitting or lying and you're calm, relaxed, and aren't ill, your heart rate is normally between 60 (beats per minute) and 100 (beats per minute).

To keep a healthy heart, you need to eat right, exercise, and protect it.

Here are seven things you can do to maintain a happy heart in business/life:

-Find your passion

-Make money

-Help others

-Give back

-Surround yourself with people who want you to win.

-Understand that failures, heartbreaks, and mishaps will make your heart stronger over time.

-Show appreciation to those who help you succeed.

Life is a complex puzzle, but if you have a strong heart, you can put it together to create a beautiful masterpiece.

A MOM'S LOVE NEVER ENDS. IT JUST GROWS STRONGER

The moment each of you was born changed my life forever. I'm better because of you (Collin, Gavin & Rian).

As babies, you were precious and sweet. Cute little hands and feet.

Your poopy diapers and milk spew didn't change a thing.

As a youth, your stinky uniforms hung out the window, but I enjoyed every moment still.

Teens came with puberty, and tons of laughs as we figured it out together.

As years went by, you grew into young men who will utilize your skills and talents to make an impact. Your journey into adulthood will come with peaks and valleys, but live it with intention.

As adults, I have some advice for you.

☼Always treat people with kindness. Recognize the needs around you.

♥Keep your hearts open to do good.

▦Be patient with love. If you get hurt, don't be afraid to love again.

⚜ Be selfless and give back.

🏰Strive for more than you think you can accomplish.

💪Strength comes from within, so believe in yourself.

💡 Use your knowledge to improve the world.

✅Overcome your fears to march towards your own version of greatness.

😃Only compare yourself to yourself to improve each day.

📚Learn from the hard times and become stronger.

Ⅼess phone time, more human interactions.

Ⅼive life to the fullest every second.

Ⅽreate a healthy balance of work, fun, love, and social responsibility.

Ⅼositive mindsets are within your control.

Pray daily. Love God. Love yourself even through times you might not be proud of.

Appreciate the good times, people who contribute to your life, and leaders who are a good influence.

Thank those who deserve it.

Remember that every single choice you make is important.

Call those you love. Tell them you love them and never have regrets.

You have one life to live. Live it big, bold, and selfless.

Enjoy good music, food, and fitness.

Obey the law.

Respect your elders.

I love you unconditionally and forever. No matter where you are or where I am, I'm with you, and you are with me... forever!

-Mom

What does QB mean?

A: Quarterback. I want to help you strategize to win in life and business. Let's all create our own plays to score many touchdowns. My brand found me after I started doing motivational speaking. Little did I know, I was living out my brand the day I started putting others first. Instead of focusing on my needs, I started focusing on making others around me smile. Someone in the audience recognized that and said, "You're kinda like the quarterback of people's lives," to which I humbly replied, "Yes, that's true. I love helping people score their own touchdowns!" It stuck from that day forward.

Q/A with QB Darla

How many times should you try to call someone to make a sale?

A: As many times as it takes.

How do you maintain a positive mindset? Positive in = positive out. Surround yourself with good content, positive news, and encouraging people. Learn daily. Laugh often.

I want to believe in myself, but I struggle. How can I get past that?

A: Realize that everyone has unique talents and gifts. Then, put in the work. Change your routine to work smarter and harder. Show up. Find hobbies outside of work, such as music, reading, nature, travel, social groups, family, and exercise.

Life is hard. How do I adapt to big changes?

A: Every person handles change differently. Dig deep to embrace change and welcome new opportunities. A lot of successful people have failed first, learned from it, and then kept pushing forward.

How do you get up every morning and stay upbeat?

A: When you train your brain to rise and grind for a specific purpose, you can't wait to get up and work hard. Find your purpose!

How do you drive yourself to reach your goals?

A: Visualize results and what you want to do with your earnings. Then, visualize your legacy and what you will be leaving behind. Treasures are how hard you work, the impact you make, and the things you overcome that create your own unique story. Everyone's journey is different. Start saying, "When I...not If I..."

Now, go throw a touchdown and bet on yourself to win the game!

CONCLUSION CHAPTER

As we wrap up these final pages of the road where you and I have been walking together, I don't want to simply move you with motivation; I want to leave you with the truth. Not chin-up surface encouragement, but a heart-to-heart reminder of all that you already have inside. It's a new chapter for you to embark on. It's time for your brand, legacy, and voice to begin.

You Already Have a Personal Brand

Let's begin here: you have a personal brand already. Whether you've dedicated years to building it or it struck you just now as you read this book, the fact is this: your brand is what stands between you and the world outside. It's how you wear what you've been through, what holds you down, and what lifts you up. It's the electricity that fills a room when you walk in and the sense of loss when you walk out. You don't need to be perfect. You don't need millions of followers or a perfect logo. You only have to be yourself, all the way and unapologetically. Because no one else on this earth can bring to the table the combination of strengths, insights, and lived experiences that you can! That's your superpower. Visibility and recognition are not the beginning and end of your personal brand. It's about authenticity. It's about showing up as the person you truly are, not just who the world expects you to be. Whether you're a coach, an artist, a businesswoman, a mother, a father, or all of the above, your story matters. Your voice matters. And your presence? It's powerful beyond measure. Just be you!

Know Your Worth

So many of us shrink to fit inside boxes we were never meant to enter. We oftentimes play small just to make others comfortable. But let me remind you of something: you are worthy, not because of what you produce or how much you achieve, but because of who you are at your core. In your heart, know that you are irreplaceable because God didn't create anyone else like you. When you understand your value, everything shifts. You stop waiting for permission. You stop chasing validation. You stop dimming your light to keep others from feeling insecure. You were not born to be background noise in someone else's story; you were always meant to shine and have your own limelight. Be bold. Be brave. Go after what you want. Let fear walk with you, but don't let it lead you. Your dreams deserve your full attention, your gallant efforts, and your most authentic voice. You weren't meant to survive—you were meant to thrive.

Grow and Give

Branding is not just about growing a platform; it is about creating a meaningful impact. It's easy to get caught up in the metrics: likes, follows, sales, and recognition. And while money and influence are important tools, they are not the destination; they are only vehicles. They're meant to help you reach wider with your message.

So, define your brand. Get clear on your mission. Grow your platform intentionally. And then? Use it for good. Use it to speak truth, to uplift others, to advocate for change, and to pour light into dark places. When you

build a platform with purpose, you begin to live beyond yourself.

Fulfillment doesn't come from status—it comes from service. True happiness is rooted in giving back, in lifting others as you climb, and in using your influence to heal, to build, to transform.

Take that action

No one starts something new feeling 100% ready. Fear whispers lies like "You're not enough," "You're too late," or "You'll fail." But guess what? Fear doesn't get the final say. Action does.

It's okay to feel afraid; that's what makes us human. What matters is what you do with it. Use that fear as fuel. Let it push you, stretch you, even humble you—but never let it paralyze you or halt your growth. Your greatness isn't waiting for fear to go away; it's waiting for you to move forward anyway. Take the leap of faith. Start the business. Launch the brand. Make the call. Write the book. Send the pitch. Get it done. And remember, done is better than perfect. Growth only happens in motion.

It's Never Too Late

Maybe you're just starting this journey at 30. Or maybe you're 50 and wondering if the right moment has passed. Let me assure you—it hasn't. It's never too late to make a positive impact. As long as you're breathing, there's time to build, to inspire, to create, and to live fully.

Reinvention is a gift, not a flaw. Life is constantly giving you the chance to start fresh, to step into your purpose in a new way. Don't let age, circumstance, or past mistakes fool you into thinking your best days are behind you. Remind yourself that the best days are ahead of you. You just have to be willing to claim them.

The Final Word

If you remember nothing else from this book, remember this: You matter. Your voice matters. Your presence matters.

You were born with a purpose. The world is waiting—not for some polished, perfected version of you,

but for the real you. The brave you. The vulnerable, beautiful, gifted you.

Don't let doubt steal your vocation. Don't let comparison rob your joy. You were never meant to follow someone else's script; you were always meant to write your own destiny.

At the end of the day, the goal isn't just success—it's significance. It's not just building a name. It's building a legacy.

And you, my friend, are more than capable.

Now, go out there and show the world who you really are.

Best Wishes,

Please engage with QB Darla as a speaker or author at:

https://qbdarla.com/

To order books, visit:

https://wittypublications.com/